THE CONSCRIPTION CRISIS OF 1944

THE CONSCRIPTION

CRISIS OF 1944

by R. MacGregor Dawson

UNIVERSITY OF TORONTO PRESS

University of Toronto Press

Diamond Anniversary 1961

note

In 1951 Professor R. MacG. Dawson took up residence in Ottawa to begin his work as official biographer of William Lyon Mackenzie King. He had only started to make his way through the voluminous material collected by his subject when a critically important event in the career of the late Prime Minister suddenly received new and fervent discussion in the press. This event was the conscription crisis of 1944, and the renewal of debate was occasioned by the publication in 1952 of Bruce Hutchison's book *The Incredible Canadian.*

The revival of the issue in its pages and in the public prints took on a special immediacy as most of the participants of 1944 were still alive and available for comment. Professor Dawson seized the opportunity to interview and analyse, and he set down his findings in three draft chapters. These, possibly somewhat revised, would eventually have taken their place in the biography proper had he lived to complete it, but regrettably he died just before the first volume, taking the story to 1923, had been published. The Literary Executors of Mackenzie King, Professor Dawson's family, and his publisher have felt that the three chapters on conscription, containing some of his most vigorous writing and forming a narrative complete in themselves, should now be made available to his many readers in book form.

contents

THE CONSCRIPTION CRISIS OF 1944

THE *first* PHASE

Until the late summer of 1944 the people and Government of Canada had every reason to view with satisfaction the progress of the war and their own part in the general endeavour. The invasion of Italy had not gone as smoothly as had been anticipated; but on the other hand the landing in Normandy had been brilliantly successful and had been attended with relatively light casualties, France had been virtually all reclaimed, the enemy had been driven out of Belgium and his grip on Holland was being broken, while the central stronghold of Germany was being invested from east and west. Final victory, it seemed evident, could not be long postponed. At the Quebec Conference in September representatives of the British and United States Governments were chiefly concerned with the war against Japan, and the same topic engaged the attention of the Canadian Cabinet and the British delegation in a joint meeting on September 14. Thus while the Canadian Navy still patrolled the Atlantic and the Canadian forces were heavily engaged in Italy and Holland, the end—at least so far as the European hostilities were concerned—was in sight. In early October the Canadian Government was considering what arrangements should be made for celebrating V-Day.*

It was in this atmosphere of imminent success and relaxed tension that the ghost of conscription once more made its sudden and quite unexpected re-appearance. The 1942 visitation had caused uneasiness and even alarm throughout the country; but the proper measures had been taken and the incantation of "Conscription if necessary, but not necessarily conscription" had been sufficiently potent to cause the spectre to dissolve and vanish. There were a few who from time to time had foretold that another manifestation was impending, but these were mostly alarmists and trouble-makers who were generally considered to be unreliable and to have derived a peculiar and sadistic satisfaction from the horrid apparition of 1942. Events proved, however, that the gloomy prophecies of this group were only too accurate. Canada, it seemed, lay under a wartime curse which decreed that the conscription issue was bound to arise to confound and convulse the nation. The labours and sorrows of war must be rendered yet more oppressive by the threat of an underlying schism, one which not only would cripple the national war effort, but would set people against people, province against province, not for the duration of the war alone, but for many years to come.

*[Opposite this paragraph in the manuscript is written in Dr. Dawson's hand: "This is inaccurate and will be altered." It is altogether likely that he would have altered the concluding part of his second sentence to read in some such words as these: 'but on the other hand the landing in Normandy had been brilliantly successful and had been attended with casualties lighter than had been anticipated, France had been virtually all reclaimed, the enemy had been driven out of most of Belgium and his grip on Holland was being threatened, while the central stronghold of Germany was being invested from east and west.'—EDITORIAL NOTE.]

The Canadian effort during the five years of war had been impressive, and the record of voluntary enlistments was one of its most conspicuous features. More than 500,000 men had enlisted in the army, some 200,000 in the air force, and about 75,000 in the navy.[1] The device of calling up men for home defence under the National Resources Mobilization Act had worked surprisingly well, especially as an indirect method of obtaining "volunteers": almost 60,000 N.R.M.A. men were serving in Canada at the end of October, 1944, with 8,000 others on extended leave, while some 42,000 more (included in the half million above) had enlisted in the active army, and almost 6,000 had gone into other fighting services.[2] The stream of army recruits, however, was beginning to dry up and the total number of volunteers as well as those drawn from N.R.M.A. ranks fell off perceptibly during the summer of 1944. The total of voluntary enlistments for June was 6,282 (including 2,976 N.R.M.A. men); for August 5,256 (1,350 N.R.M.A.); for October, 4,710 (848 N.R.M.A.).[3] These figures, however, caused no alarm at Ottawa, for the military advisers of the Government had given the assurance again and again that the men available were ample to meet all demands.[4] Thus while the Canadian overseas headquarters reported in June that unexpectedly heavy casualties had made larger reinforcing drafts necessary in the future, various adjustments were considered sufficient to meet the need, notably an agreement by the three Defence Ministers (Ralston, Power, Macdonald)* to slow down navy and air force recruiting in order to help the army fill its quota of volunteers.[5] J. L. Ralston, the Minister of National Defence, was thus able in the following month to announce that there were on hand "sufficient general service men to complete our quotas right up to the calendar year end."[6] In

*See the list of Cabinet Ministers on p. 131.

early August the Chief of Staff (Canadian Military Headquarters Overseas) reiterated that the over-all reinforcement
position was entirely satisfactory,[7] and although some difficulties were encountered a few weeks later, these were
treated as only temporary problems and the Staff in Europe
professed to be quite satisfied.[8] A cable to this effect was sent
to Ottawa but it was simply read and initialled by the
Minister, who failed to grasp its portentous character. He
regarded it as merely a routine matter and did not consider it
of sufficient importance to report to the Cabinet.[9] In September, when plans for future operations in the Pacific were
being made at the Quebec Conference, the Canadian army
chiefs who were present gave no sign that they were in any
way uneasy about the existing supply of troops. "Nothing
was said at that time," said Mackenzie King in the House
some months later, "which could give any member of the
Government of Canada reason to believe that we were near-
ing the time, or that we were fearing the time, when it might
be necessary to resort to conscription to provide men for
service overseas as reinforcements to our army."[10]

This feeling of security was shattered in the next few
weeks by disclosures which confronted the Cabinet with a
crisis of the first magnitude. The newspapers began to carry
stories of poorly trained reinforcements, convalescent soldiers
returned to the front before they had made a complete re-
covery, and other reports of a disquieting nature. The
Government, relying on the optimistic cables from its military advisers, was at first incredulous, but when Ralston
received a further report from overseas headquarters on the
number of available reinforcements for the infantry, he
became alarmed. He informed the War Committee of the
Cabinet of some of his misgivings and a few days later, at
the end of September, left on his annual trip to Europe
determined to investigate the actual situation for himself.

He was to be speedily enlightened. When he began his inquiry in Italy a cynical officer is reported to have asked
whether he desired to hear the official story or the truth, and
the truth proved to be even worse than he had feared.[11] The
pools from which the essential infantry reinforcements were
drawn were almost exhausted and the reserves in sight were
insufficient to make up the deficiency. The supply in northwestern Europe was no better. The military authorities had
been, of course, quite aware of the situation, but they had
apparently been gambling on a speedy termination of the war
and a consequent lessening in the demand for troops.
Whether they had been trying to shield the Government and
make the best of the existing system, or had been protecting
themselves from the consequences of their own earlier errors
of judgment, or, more subtly, had been hoping to discredit
the Government's policy—is here of little moment. The
responsible officers should at least have informed their Minister of the chances they were taking. In not doing so, they not
only betrayed him, they precipitated a national crisis which
might have been avoided had the basic facts been disclosed
in time to allow adequate measures to be taken along the
established lines of the Government's policy.

The Minister of National Defence broke his trip short
and brought the Chief of Staff, General K. Stuart, with him
to Ottawa to present a report to the Cabinet. It disclosed that
although the army drafts from Canada had been kept up to
the allotted quota, these had not been sufficient to replace the
casualties. In all branches except the infantry the losses were
less than those which had been anticipated and the supply of
reinforcements was more than adequate; but while the infantry casualties were expected to work out at 45 per cent of
the total for the whole army, they had in fact been about 75
per cent. The forecast was based on probability tables prepared and used by the British War Office, and similar mis-

calculations had been made by the United States forces. The Canadian army staff may have derived some consolation from the fact that other nations also erred in their estimates, but this did little to relieve their acute problem overseas or to avert the embarrassing consequences to the Government at home. The infantry reinforcement pools were being steadily depleted. The French-speaking battalions had at this time virtually no reserves whatever, and Canadians with French names although often completely ignorant of the French language were being hastily transferred into these units to fill the gaps. All pools had been partly replenished during the past months by a re-mustering programme which had diverted men from other arms of the service into the infantry, but this device had very obvious limits. While there were few cases of insufficiently trained reinforcements being used, men were being sent back to the front lines before they had fully recovered from their wounds; a large number in Italy had been serving for over four years without home leave; the troops were dissatisfied and morale was beginning to suffer. Fifteen thousand additional infantry were required to bring the establishments up to normal in the United Kingdom and on the Continent, and in the opinion of the Minister and his military advisers these could be obtained only by the conscription of the N.R.M.A. men for overseas service.[12]

These representations were given in outline by the Minister to Mackenzie King on October 18 and in detail to the War Committee on the following day. All members were shocked at the disclosures and alarmed at their implications, for it was evident that if the men had to be secured by conscription the consequences would be very serious indeed. No one was more concerned than the Prime Minister. His whole political life, like that of Laurier, had been centred on the effort to bind together French and English Canada, and he was thus a confirmed anti-conscriptionist so long as that policy could be applied with any hope of success. In the renewal of the demand for conscription at this time, King saw the possible destruction of all the good accomplished in the last twenty years. His Government had maintained the Canadian war effort at a high level, and although there had been difficulties in 1942 the plebiscite and the temporizing policy of Bill 80* had proved adequate and had been accepted by all but the extremists on both sides. Now, after five years of war with an assured victory in sight, the issue was suddenly revived. While the major as well as the immediate blame could fairly be placed on military shoulders, the Government could not be absolved of all responsibility, especially in helping to create the basic conditions which underlay the crisis. The chief political offenders were clearly Ralston and King. Both had been too prone to accept the opinion of their military experts; both had failed to block the "big army" idea in its early stages; both had allowed themselves to be persuaded by the officers that manpower resources of the nation would be sufficient to meet the united demands of the armed forces and the equally vital civilian war activities. The reinforcement crisis demonstrated that there were not enough men to go round, unless, indeed, much more effective use could be made of those who were already nominally in the armed forces, or a further element of compulsion was introduced to send more men overseas.

*[By the plebiscite of April 1942 a decisive "Yes" was returned to the question: "Are you in favour of releasing the Government from any obligation arising out of any past commitments restricting the methods of raising men for military service?" Subsequently, by the passage of Bill 80, the National Resources Mobilization Act, which had instituted compulsory service for home defence only, was amended; the Government could now by Order-in-Council send N.R.M.A. men overseas, but these full powers had so far been held in reserve.—EDITORIAL NOTE.]

King fully appreciated many of the difficulties which lay ahead, but his confidence in his ability to produce a solution remained undiminished. His diary for October 18 gives this analysis:

It is tragic that this situation should arise at this time, when the party's fortunes are steadily rising and the country in a mood to see the war through in a noble way. To me it is about as heavy a task as could be given to a man to bear for whatever decision is made I shall be the one that will be pilloried on the one side by the Army and its friends, if I do not yield to what in the long run would not be in its interests and certainly at no time in the interests of Canada, and on the other hand by the great majority of the people of Canada itself if, after the stand I have taken right along and with such success, I should permit a situation to develop that will help to destroy the unity of Canada for years to come and that to no avail so far as the winning of the war is concerned. Ralston did say it was not the winning of the war that was at stake. To my mind that is the only stake on which we are justified on [in?] sacrificing more lives than may be absolutely necessary. I do feel that the position of the war at the moment is such that the certainty of defeat of Germany is possible in a short time and that it will not be possible for Ralston to carry the Cabinet with him and that he certainly would not carry Parliament if called, as it would have to be, before such a step were taken unless the issue were made one for a general election. The shame is that there should have to be any issue at this time. I believe that we shall get through without conscription and that the same power which has guided me in the past will continue to guide me through another very difficult period.[18]

King accepted for the most part the basic facts submitted by Ralston and his Chief of Staff, but in the War Committee and later in the Cabinet he attacked the proposed remedy as inadvisable and probably unnecessary. Conscription for overseas service, he emphasized, could not be applied without a political upheaval. Parliament, which had adjourned in August, would have to be called, a bitter debate would ensue, and almost certainly a general election would follow. The country would be split on the question, and there would be a residue of hatred like that which had remained after the First World War. When it was suggested that there would be no necessity for an election, he replied that the demand in Parliament and the country would probably be so insistent that it might prove inevitable. The intervention of an election, moreover, would be sure to interfere with the dispatch of troops; the contest would take over two months, and little could be done until the nation had made its pronouncement. Enemy morale would be improved by news of disagreements in Canada, and Canada's later war effort against Japan would in all likelihood be crippled by the conscription dispute. Empire relations might also be affected adversely, for the movement to take Canada out of the Commonwealth would be strengthened by the argument that Canada went into this war in large measure because of the United Kingdom and could then maintain her army in the field only by a resort to force.

It could not be contended for a moment, he argued, that the outcome of the war would be influenced by Canada's inability to send over a few thousand more men. The war was virtually over; indeed, if there were an election, an armistice might even be signed before the voters got to the polls. The purpose of introducing conscription at this time would be to keep the army up to strength, yet it was doubtful if this was essential. Germany was weakening, and recruits from the lately occupied countries in Europe were augmenting the forces of the United Nations. Moreover, when the British and American armies had found themselves in precisely the same difficulty of inadequate reinforcements, they had met the emergency by turning a number of active units into reinforcing drafts.

Nor, King continued, could the Government neglect its own future as a party and its reconstruction programme. There was no assurance that if the Government stood behind conscription, an election would return it to power. Even if it were returned, its measures of reconstruction and of social legislation would suffer in the post-war years, which would furnish problems enough without the additional bitterness conscription would carry over into that period.

Ralston's position had at least the virtue of simplicity, and in him the Department of National Defence had an eloquent and sincere spokesman. He contended that in fairness to the men who had served and were serving in the army the overseas units must be maintained at full strength, and any suggestion of a reduction in the establishments could not be considered as long as trained N.R.M.A. men were available. He had always looked upon the home army as a reserve for the one overseas, and the time had come to use it. The possibilities of the voluntary system were exhausted, and there was only one way now to turn. "Conscription if necessary" Ralston asserted had always meant "necessary to maintain the Canadian army" and not, as the Prime Minister contended, "necessary to win the war." To lessen the war effort now was to go back on the Canadian forces in action and, in effect, repudiate the sacrifices which had already been made.

After three meetings of the War Committee the matter was referred to the full Cabinet on October 24 for discussion and action. It was clear that although the men immediately involved in Ralston's recommendation were few in number, they bulked large when related to those who were able and willing to serve; and their procurement thus presented the most controversial issue to face a Canadian Cabinet in a generation. The 1942 crisis had been met by a compromise, but there seemed to be no compromise available here. The question, however, had appeared so suddenly that no final decision could be taken until the situation had been thoroughly investigated and all possible alternatives considered. "I feel," King wrote in his diary on the first day of the discussion (October 19), "there is everything to be gained by time," and he was not disposed to hurry the Cabinet to a premature commitment.

Ralston's case rested on the assumptions that the war would last for an indefinite period and that the Canadian army would continue to be engaged as actively in the future as in the past. If these could be disproved, Ralston's case would be greatly weakened and a crisis averted. To get the facts at the highest strategic level King promptly cabled Churchill. After reviewing the existing political situation in Canada caused by the re-emergence of the conscription issue, he asked two fundamental questions: (1) What was the probable duration of the war in Europe? (2) Were the Canadians likely to be engaged in the next major action? When a reply was not immediately forthcoming, King intimated privately to Malcolm Macdonald, the British High Commissioner, that his need for an answer was most urgent, and Macdonald on his own responsibility sent a further report to England on the existing situation. Churchill's reply arrived the following day. It was: (1) that the war in Europe might be expected to go on until mid-summer, 1945; (2) that the Canadian army would undoubtedly be engaged in further large-scale operations, but its use in the immediate future was still uncertain.

Obviously, these answers did nothing to deny the validity of Ralston's assumptions, and if disclosed to the Cabinet would, on the contrary, have greatly strengthened the position of the conscriptionists. King therefore kept his own counsel.* He had, it is true, mentioned to his colleagues a few days before that he was thinking of communicating with both Churchill and Roosevelt to obtain additional information. He was not, however, unaware of the possibility of a damaging reply, and he had therefore deliberately omitted to inform his colleagues that any approach to Churchill had been attempted. The nature of the reply, when it came, made it impossible for King to use the opinion of Churchill and the British Chief of Staff to support his own contention that it was folly at this advanced stage in the war to resort to an expedient which would have such disruptive effects in Canada. King made no similar inquiry of Roosevelt. Several weeks later he did ask General Maurice Pope, who was in Washington for another purpose, to call on the President and acquaint him with recent developments in Canada. There is no evidence that Pope's interview elicited any significant response.

The War Committee and the Cabinet wrestled with the problem from October 19 to November 1, but made little progress. Everyone wished, if possible, to continue voluntary enlistment, but a number of the Ministers agreed with Ralston that this method would no longer produce the men and would therefore result in a slackening in the war effort. Many had always believed that conscription was the only

---

*The Cabinet were not long in ignorance, however, of the probable length of the war. King received Churchill's reply on October 27. Four days later Churchill told Parliament: "On military grounds it seems difficult to believe that the war could be ended before Christmas, or even before Easter, although . . . many high military authorities with every means to form a correct judgment have expressed themselves more hopefully." *Br. H. of C. Debates*, Oct. 31, 1944, p. 663.

just system, though perhaps not the wisest, and there was a growing conviction among many of the English-speaking members that Quebec's susceptibilities had received more than fair consideration during the past five years. The longer the Cabinet debated, the more rigid became the convictions of the participants and the more definitely did they split into conscriptionist and anti-conscriptionist divisions. King exerted his pressure, mildly but inflexibly, in favour of continuing the existing system.

All the Cabinet discussions were conducted with an even temper and with a sincere desire to arrive at a solution. Thus although the three Defence Ministers were divided, with Ralston and Macdonald believing that the time had come to adopt conscription for overseas service and Power wishing to retain the existing system, they were united by a warm affection and a friendship which never faltered at any time during these critical weeks. Similarly, the French-speaking members of the Cabinet could count on the sympathy and understanding of virtually all their colleagues; and neither the situation itself nor the disagreement which was, so it seemed, the inevitable result of that situation, gave rise to any reproaches or personal animosity.

A notable exception to this general goodwill was the feeling which some Ministers entertained towards the Prime Minister and, to a somewhat lesser degree, the Prime Minister's feeling towards them, though even between these the discussions were carried on amicably and without heat. Crerar, Ilsley, Ralston, and Macdonald had by this time become convinced conscriptionists, and they found in King's stubborn refusal to abandon the voluntary system further evidence to confirm a suspicion which had been growing in their minds since the crisis of 1942. They believed that King could not be relied on, and that come what might, he would never, despite what he had said, accept overseas conscription under any circumstances.

This interpretation did less than justice to the Prime Minister, whose views had been succinctly but somewhat ambiguously expressed in the phrase "conscription if necessary." What meaning was to be placed on these words? His own understanding of "necessary," King maintained, had always been "necessary to win the war," although now that the war was virtually won, it was evident that the phrase could have little if any force when applied to such circumstances as those confronting the Cabinet at this time. It is true that he had allowed his Ministers, and especially Ralston, to read the meaning they desired into these words without feeling any obligation to correct them, and he cannot altogether escape some blame for his silence. It is also true that he had, on one earlier occasion at least,[14] given "the maintenance of the necessary reinforcements for Canada's army overseas" as an example of the condition which "would render the use of compulsion imperative." There seems, however, to be little real doubt that here, as at other times when he spoke of procuring the required number of troops, he was contemplating a crisis of such gravity that the maintenance of the army would be absolutely vital to the Canadian war effort. Such a contingency would have arisen, for example, had the landing in Normandy been attended by casualties so heavy that large reinforcements would have been imperative to sustain the Canadian army as an effective fighting force. Under these circumstances, King told Parliament in November 1944, "I would not have lost one hour in bringing this House of Commons together and asking hon. members to support the Government in sending the needed reinforcements at once, and I believe those reinforcements would have been granted without any division in this House."[15] Even a casual examination of King's speeches will disclose that when he used the word "necessity" in connection with conscription he associated it with such conditions as "the security of our country," "urgent necessity," "risk of invasion and conquest," "great danger," "hour of emergency," "time of peril," "preservation of the national existence," "the preservation of freedom." These give a much more accurate idea of the kind of situation which King thought would warrant compulsion. Only the gravest danger could justify risking the damage which he was convinced conscription would be bound to inflict on the unity of the nation.

King had always insisted, moreover, that the Government must keep its hands free to make its decision on conscription "in the light of all relevant circumstances" and that the maintenance of the war effort meant a balanced and not a one-sided participation. "The achievement of a total effort involves much more than the raising of large numbers of men," he said in 1942. "It involves the most effective use of all the available resources of the nation, material as well as human. . . . It is not merely a question of raising men for the army, which was the main problem in the last war."[16] The gain of a few extra men in the army might be offset many times by internal dissension and a consequent loss in other fields of national endeavour. "Compulsion, in any form, should be used in the war effort only if it will make Canada stronger, and add to Canada's part in winning the war."[17]

It was therefore not true, as some of his colleagues believed, that King was unalterably opposed under any circumstances to the introduction of conscription for overseas service. There is even some reason to suppose that conscription presented King with a personal problem of social justice quite apart from the political conflicts which the issue inevitably engendered and for which he could provide no clear or certain answer. He thus could not fail to appreciate the moral imperative of equal sacrifice, but he was also appalled by the eagerness with which unscrupulous persons were prepared to use their country's extremity as a pretext for imposing their own views on others and placing upon their opponents the stigma of indifference and even of moral turpitude. As a political leader, moreover, he could never forget the unhappy experience of 1917, and he was determined to do all in his power to avoid a repetition. But if an emergency arose and conscription became "necessary and advisable," he was quite prepared to take the step: the risk of endangering national unity might then have to be taken in order to safeguard the nation's existence. In such circumstances opposition to conscription would probably vanish before the overriding menace of a more obvious and more serious danger. But the demand for troops in October 1944, while it was alarming enough, did not arise from any threat to the national safety, and King, whether he was right or wrong, was quite consistent when he refused to take the responsibility for the adoption of conscription under the circumstances existing at that time.

The scepticism with which certain of his Ministers received King's pronouncements on conscription was unhappily enhanced by a statement which he was alleged to have made at a luncheon given by the Quebec Reform Club on September 14, 1944. The war at this time was progressing satisfactorily, the danger of overseas conscription appeared to have passed, and the Prime Minister was not averse to calling Quebec's attention to his skilful generalship in avoiding this issue in its most troublesome form. Ministers who heard his address reported that he announced that he had never believed in conscription and that if it should hereafter become imperative, he himself would not enforce it, but would retire and let someone else take the responsibility. The Minister of National Defence was not at the luncheon, and when on the following day he asked King about the speech and whether it indicated a change in policy he was told that the statement had been directed solely at operations in the Pacific and was not applicable and had never been intended to apply to the war in Europe. The luncheon was a private one and the exact reference has not been recorded, but at least three of the Ministers present refused to accept King's denial. They insisted that his pronouncement had nothing whatever to do with the Pacific and that it was designed to consolidate his position in Quebec which had been rendered somewhat uncertain by the 1942 legislation. When the crisis occurred some weeks after the Reform Club incident, the conscriptionist Ministers not unnaturally took the statement as a confirmation of their opinion that King would not take what was to them the inevitable step towards overseas conscription.

Another element in the situation was the fact that Mackenzie King was never a military man in any sense: his distrust of the army was deep-seated and life-long. His inclination was to blame it now—not without reason—for the Government's predicament. Three years before the 1944 crisis he was convinced that unless it was carefully watched the ambition of the military officers was likely to lead the Cabinet into difficulties. He noted in his diary:

I think our whole problem with respect to the whole cause of the issue of conscription becoming a vital one is due to the Defence Departments and, in particular, the army. One might almost say exclusively the army, pushing its establishment too rapidly to the fore. They have aimed at an army overseas, not wanting one large Corps but 2 Corps so as to make an army, and have virtually brought matters to a pass where to complete that programme, and to have the necessary reserves, the issue of conscription necessarily arises.[18]

Yet the Cabinet, including, of course, the Prime Minister, had acquiesced in this very questionable policy, and they had allowed themselves to be overborne by the urgent enthusiasm of the soldiers, who, so far as is known, had never at any time in any place advocated a small army if there was any conceivable chance of obtaining a large one. What reliance could the Cabinet place on an *ex parte* plea for expansion put forward by men whose instincts, training, and ambition all favoured larger and larger forces, and who were notoriously ignorant of and indifferent to the political consequences which might follow? Lesser proposals which in the long run yielded the same general result tended to follow the same course. The Prime Minister and the Cabinet would demur, the military advisers would insist that the supply of men was more than ample, and the politicians would eventually give way to the advice of the experts. Only two months before the crisis of 1944 developed, General Stuart had stated when submitting one of these proposals that although it would involve some additional replacements for casualties, this was a risk which in the existing situation he was quite prepared to assume. No one seemed to be very clear what the acceptance of such a risk really involved in terms of responsibility. Politically, it meant, and could mean, nothing; and the Cabinet was left to face the consequences and to devise means of extricating the army—and itself—from the trying situation thus created. It was inevitable that some Ministers should reflect that in this crisis they were once more relying on the military advice of officers who had already been proved wrong in their estimated requirements for men and had also been shown to be unreliable in their dealings with their Minister.

The chief responsibility for all military matters rested, of course, on the Minister of National Defence. Ralston was in many ways an exceptionally fine type of cabinet minister. He had had a distinguished record as commander of a battalion and later of a brigade in the First World War, and the bonds of respect and affection then established between him and his men continued unbroken through the years. Honest, forthright, sincere, his qualities had won the admiration and high regard of all with whom he came in contact. He was completely dependable either as a colleague in the Cabinet or as the head of a department, and he was fearless in the discharge of what he conceived to be his duty. His earlier war services had given him a very close sympathy with the army in the field, and he always regarded himself in his ministerial capacity as being pre-eminently the spokesman and pleader for the ordinary soldier. When he thought of the army he thought of the private who had told him of his troubles a few weeks before, of the wounded he had talked to in the hospitals, of the courage, *esprit de corps*, and other fine characteristics which he knew from experience were evoked by exposure to common dangers on the battlefield.[19]

It is difficult to quarrel with human qualities of so admirable a kind, but they furnish a clue to one or two of Ralston's outstanding weaknesses. He became unduly absorbed in the minutiae of administration. He attempted to do too many things himself rather than delegate them to subordinates, an immersion in detail which was administratively possible only because of his tremendous energy and capacity for unremitting toil. This characteristic when joined to his well-known sympathy for the common soldier had unfortunate consequences. He tended to devote too much attention to immediate and transitory grievances of a minor kind to the exclusion of far more vital matters. He was unusually vulnerable to proposals put forward by his senior advisers which would be likely to improve the lot or prospects of the soldier in the field. While Ralston could be and often was tough and unyielding with his officers, he was himself too much of a soldier to be able to regard the army with the critical detachment which a highly efficient Minister must possess if he is to exercise general control at all times. Suspicion of expert and pseudo-expert advice and the ability to scrutinize the knowledge and outlook behind it, are necessary qualities in any Minister; they are absolutely indispensable when dealing with the closed and intolerant hierarchies of the armed services.

This natural but unusually powerful bias in favour of his department had its effect on Ralston's relations with the Cabinet and his attitude to Cabinet policy. He was not, perhaps, sufficiently sensitive in distinguishing between that which might be militarily desirable and that which was politically feasible. His zeal for the welfare of his men was apt to dim his appreciation of the extent to which his colleagues or the country could be induced to follow his lead. Thus Mackenzie King complained in his diary during the conscription crisis that Ralston's vision was limited to the achievement of his immediate purpose and that he had little comprehension of the wider issues which the whole question of compulsion inevitably raised.[20] Because of this, Ralston was apt to oversimplify his problems, a characteristic which no doubt added strength and drive to the work of his department, but was bound, sooner or later, to prove a disruptive force in the Council chamber.

Ralston's high degree of concentration on the welfare

and safety of his army also gave an inflexibility to his determination to send more reinforcements and made him impatient of any delay. He kept hammering away in the Cabinet at the problem, bringing the discussion back to the main issue, pressing for action, and never allowing his colleagues to forget the urgency of the question and the necessity of formulating a policy to meet it. "There is," wrote King, "something inhumanly determined about his getting his own way, regardless of what the effects may be on all others."[21] This criticism was not entirely just. Ralston's outlook on the problem may have lacked perspective, but he was fighting, as any good Minister would have fought, for his department and for what he conceived to be its greatest need. Nor even here was he unreasonable in the way in which he placed his problem before the Cabinet or in his demand for a solution. He was by this time, it is true, a conscriptionist; but he was quite willing to consider and try any programme which he thought would be likely to produce the men within the time available. What he would not accept was procrastination: the problem must be squarely faced and a feasible plan—conscription or otherwise—must be produced without delay.

Day after day the War Committee and the Cabinet considered alternative methods of producing the required reinforcements within the time available, only to discard them as inadequate. Thus an accelerated training, a lowering of the age limit and of certain physical requirements, and a reversion in rank of non-commissioned officers promised to yield only a few thousand; and although more might be obtained by making overseas enlistment more attractive to N.R.M.A. troops the difference did not promise to be very substantial. A proposal that the men who were at this time being let out of the air force might be induced to re-enlist as a special branch of the infantry seemed to be feasible, but the training requirements were such that these men would not be ready soon enough to fill the existing gap. It was also suggested that the infantry battalions might be reduced from four rifle companies to three or that, as an alternative, one whole infantry division might be disbanded (as had been done in Great Britain) and used as reinforcements. Both of these proposals, however, were decisively rejected, for no one thought that the Canadian people would tolerate any deliberate diminution in the fighting strength of the army so long as there were 60,000 N.R.M.A. men in Canada, many of them fully trained and potentially available for overseas service. The N.R.M.A. device had, in short, been very useful in procuring men without squarely facing the conscription issue; but the time had come when the separate existence of the N.R.M.A. troops had become a reproach and had made any further compromises with the voluntary system very difficult to justify.

On October 25 the Cabinet discovered for the first time that there were no less than 120,000 General Service men in Canada and 90,000 more in the United Kingdom, and while about one-fifth of these were in the training stream, the great bulk were not considered to be available as reinforcements. A sub-committee of the three Defence Ministers was appointed to re-examine the possibilities of utilizing more of this General Service personnel, but the Ministers reported that very few additional recruits could be drawn from this enormous reservoir after allowance had been made for those in low medical categories, ineligible age groups, administrative staff, forestry corps, provost corps, instructors, and others. These impressive figures and the readiness with which the Cabinet sub-committee accepted the fact that nothing could be done about them form one of the unexplained mysteries of the conscription crisis. Any layman (and this, according to rumour, includes more than one Cabinet member of the time) simply cannot believe the statement that it was impossible to secure 15,000 men from a pool of 210,000, or, properly excluding those in the training stream, a pool of between 165,000 and 170,000.* The sub-committee of the Cabinet conferred with some of the top military officers, spent one evening conducting their inquiry at headquarters in Ottawa, and then decided that the army's finding, that with few exceptions these men were all unavailable, had been proved. It may be so; but the sceptic will be pardoned if he retains the conviction that a Sir Clifford Sifton or a C. D. Howe would after two weeks' work have extracted the men or the army would have lost a large number of officers. Prying men loose from the grasp of the military machine is not accomplished by examining files in Ottawa or by soft words and polite methods. Experience has shown, however, that the army can do surprising things when subjected to ruthless methods administered by men who will not accept excuses as a substitute for action; but Canada at this juncture had apparently no one who was prepared to assume so formidable an undertaking.

King resolutely maintained his confidence in the continued adequacy of the voluntary system. His confidence was not derived from any known expedient for making the system more effective but rather from his conviction that

---

*"This question of the line," writes L. S. Amery of conditions in Great Britain, "inevitably raised the perennial problem, which defeated Churchill in the last war as much as it defeated Lloyd George then, of the disproportion between the numbers at the front and the men somewhere else doing no one can ever discover what. Haig, the War Office and the Ministry of National Service all produced conflicting figures." L. S. Amery, *My Political Life* (London, 1953–5), II, 134.

it alone was politically feasible and his reluctance to face
the ominous alternative. But as one Cabinet meeting succeeded another, as scheme after scheme proved sterile, and
as the line of cleavage in the Cabinet became more and
more sharply defined, King's optimism began to weaken.
He saw that the issue might not only detach some members
of his Government, but might even lead to its overthrow.
His diary and memoranda reflect his reluctance to make a
final decision, his refusal to give any encouragement to a
policy of conscription, his ceaseless effort to find a compromise which would keep the Cabinet intact and spare the
country another struggle on the lines of 1917. His ideas
and arguments varied from day to day, and shifted with the
changing outlook and the prospects for an acceptable solution. He argued that a divided Cabinet, a ministerial resignation, or the endorsement of overseas conscription would
necessitate an explanation and an appeal to Parliament.
Under these circumstances the debate in Parliament would
be bitter and prolonged, the majority given the Government,
if it was sustained, would be small, and a general election
might have to be called. An election would, of course, delay
action for months and in the end, whichever way it went,
would prove ineffective because of the internal divisions
inevitable in such a campaign. If, however, the Cabinet
would stick together and support the existing policy of
voluntary enlistment it should be able to avoid most if not
all of these possible difficulties and would be able to send
limited reinforcements overseas more quickly than the larger
number which might eventually be raised by conscription.[22]

One of King's major problems was to keep matters sufficiently fluid that the possibility of ministerial resignations
did not reach a decisive stage. Such resignations would not
only endanger the Cabinet's existence, but would probably

be disastrous to the war effort in general and to the reinforcement situation in particular. King pleaded with Ralston, both in the Cabinet meetings and in private,[28] not to resign, but Ralston felt that he was committed by his conviction, by repeated pledges, and by the duty and special responsibility he owed to the men overseas to see that compulsion was applied in the emergency. King finally accepted this as inevitable, and his mind then turned to the double task of finding a suitable successor and of ensuring that no other dissenting Minister accompanied Ralston into retirement. Although the advocates of the voluntary system outnumbered the conscriptionists in the Cabinet by at least thirteen to eight* the quality of such men as Ilsley, Macdonald, and Crerar, in addition to Ralston, made the latter group very influential indeed.

The Prime Minister had not forgotten how he had almost lost Ralston in 1942, and in this new crisis his mind had early considered a possible revival of Ralston's threatened resignation. The day after the Minister had returned from abroad and had discussed the situation with him he began to entertain the possibility of inviting General A. G. L. McNaughton to take Ralston's place if the latter should tender his resignation. McNaughton had much to recommend him. He had a tremendous popular reputation which had not been greatly dimmed by his forced retirement in December 1943. He was still the idol of the army, and he was an ardent believer in the volunteer system not only as a device for raising troops, but also as the ideal method for producing the best fighting qualities in an army. His suita-

---

*This was King's estimate on October 31 (Diary, Oct. 31, 1944). He placed Howe with the conscriptionists which, while justified later, was doubtful at that time. The others were Ralston, Crerar, Ilsley, Macdonald, Gibson, McLarty, and Mulock.

bility was enhanced by his lack of any decided party leanings, despite the fact that the Conservatives (with their leader Bracken's concurrence) were at this very moment sounding him out as a possible new leader—a circumstance which would give his appointment as a Liberal Minister a special flavour which King could not fail to appreciate. McNaughton with his military reputation, his enthusiasm, and his belief in the cause was probably the only man in Canada who at this late date might be able to make the existing system work, and King, by appointing him, would demonstrate beyond a doubt that he had done his utmost to exhaust the possibilities of voluntary enlistment. On October 20 King discussed McNaughton's suitability with Mr. St. Laurent and secured his approval. He was confirmed in his judgment the next day when the General made a speech to students at Queen's University advocating tolerance and moderation in public affairs. "When you come, as you will, to places of authority and influence," said McNaughton, "and you face the acute issues which may divide our country part from part, may I commend this principle of action to your best thought and interest—compulsion is ruled out; we proceed by agreement, or for a time we rest content not to proceed at all."[24] "If McNaughton," King commented in his diary, "had been looking into the Council Chamber and hearing all that is taking place there, he could not have given wiser counsel. My job has been to try and proceed on that principle and try to have that principle prevail."[25]

For a week King then appears to have dismissed McNaughton from his mind and concentrated on the work of conciliation and the search for a solution which would be acceptable to the entire Cabinet. By October 31, however, agreement seemed as remote as ever. Three Ministers had in the interval mentioned McNaughton's name to him, and

King finally decided to ascertain how the General felt on the matter. He invited McNaughton to Laurier House and asked in confidence for his advice on various phases of the war situation. McNaughton was both frank and critical. He was sure that sending part of the Canadian army to Italy had been a big factor in creating the shortage of men, but he appreciated the difficulties in the way of bringing the troops to the Western front in time to meet the immediate need. He favoured a public appeal for enlistment and was confident it would produce the recruits: conscription would work irreparable harm. King told him that Ralston was likely to resign and suggested that the General was the obvious successor. After some further conversation about various adjustments in personnel which might be desirable in such a contingency, McNaughton agreed to accept the portfolio if he were needed.

That afternoon was spent by the Cabinet again going over the old ground, although McLarty came forward with a new suggestion that recruiting might continue for three or four weeks longer at an intensified rate, and that if this proved to be inadequate, conscription might then be applied. The proposal met with some support from the conscriptionists, but the Prime Minister would not agree to it. He urged, among other things, that until the strategy of the war was known it was difficult to plan ahead; for if the Canadians were pulled out of the line for an interval—and such a move was long overdue—the personnel problem would be much simplified by the stream of reinforcements catching up with the need. Ralston again told the Council that his recommendation must be to send the N.R.M.A. men overseas, but he still left the way open for a preliminary period of voluntary enlistment, the length of which was not specified. It was at this meeting that the Prime Minister asked in turn Ralston,

Macdonald, and Ilsley whether he would be willing* to take the responsibility of forming a Government. It was only a rhetorical question, for King added that he had no intention of relinquishing his post;[26] but he chose this unusual method of emphasizing the fact that he alone could maintain a stable administration and, at the same time, of bringing home to the dissatisfied Ministers the responsibility which would be theirs if they decided to resign and thereby broke up the Government. The meeting adjourned with the understanding that a decision would be made the next day.

On the morning of November 1 King sent for General McNaughton and told him that Ralston would probably not remain in the Cabinet. It was therefore appropriate to discuss future policy.

I said to the General: well, we are I think now at the final stage. Matters now have narrowed down to this. That all are agreed on an appeal as a possible means of getting the necessary men; some, as probable. Ralston, not sure at all. However he is prepared to have an appeal made but asks what is the govt.'s policy should it fail. Will we be prepared to add that if it fails, we will then pass an order-in-council extending the N.R.M.A., call Parlt. together and pass it up if need be by closure. My purpose is first to avoid an election in wartime, to avoid, above all else, an election which involves the issue of conscription at a time of war. The General interjected: you are perfectly right. I said further to avoid the necessity of having Parlt. meet unless that was imperative. It would become imperative if Ralston were to resign and there was no one I could find to take his place. I do not think it would be necessary were you to take over the Dept. of Defence. I added that the object was to get the men necessary. I stated that I wanted to avoid the issue of conscription altogether. The General said: that is right.

---

*Or, according to one informant, whether the Minister "wanted" to take the responsibility. Ralston and Macdonald gave a negative reply, Ilsley said he would have to have time to decide.

I am sure that is sound. I said my appeal is we should continue the policy that we now have and which is the mandate we received at the last election to carry on the war by voluntary enlistment for overseas. That legislation since enacted have [sic] made provision for possibility of using conscription. I thought that should all [all should?] be left as it is because I was not yet persuaded that conscription was necessary. . . .[27]

McNaughton renewed his earlier criticism of the existing military administration, and raised King's hopes by the suggestion that both the General Service and N.R.M.A. problems would yield to proper treatment.

What it seemed to him was needed was a thorough house-cleaning. That one would have to make a careful study before taking any particular action. . . . He said it was ridiculous there should be such a large number of G.S. men; that headquarters here was full of people that were doing nothing. The same was true throughout Canada. On the so-called "Zombie" situation, he said that is a problem. It will have to be dealt with but the thing to do is to get them at work somewhere. . . .There is important work to be done here which they could be employed on, but these problems have to be broken up into their component parts and dealt with one by one.[28]

Both King and McNaughton thought that to set a deadline for voluntary enlistment was to court failure by assuming it, and that the time to decide on the necessity for conscription was after the effects of the attempt were known and the changed circumstances could be appraised. They also agreed in general terms on what would justify conscription, and the Prime Minister took particular care to remove any ambiguity on what his own position was on the matter:

I said: General, let me make perfectly clear what I mean about the need for conscription. I have always used it in reference to the winning of the war, not in reference to keeping the army formations up to strength. I would not want to be understood as considering conscription as necessary in any other sense but if it were necessary to win the war, I would not hesitate to put it into force. The General replied: That is correct. I mean if the situation were such that we were in real danger, danger of the enemy getting the better of us. He did not use those words but something to that effect. It was equivalent to if there were a supreme necessity, that is what I mean. He had said earlier: this must be considered in relation to the unity of Canada and what conscription would mean for or against maintaining that unity. I made it clear that there could be no mistake that I would not consider conscription in any relationship other than that of winning of the war. That was the interpretation that I had always given to it. The General said I would not regard the keeping of formations up to strength as a necessary thing. . . .

I must not forget to mention that he stressed the fact that between now and a month hence when we would be committing ourselves to introduce conscription [if Ralston's advice were followed] the whole thing might greatly change, and the need be met in other ways or be entirely removed. That he felt was the strongest of reasons for not committing oneself to any course in the intervening time.[29]

At noon King went to Rideau Hall and told the Earl of Athlone, the Governor-General, that Ralston was likely to refuse to go along with Government policy, and that if he resigned, Ilsley and Macdonald might leave with him. King advised that Ralston's resignation should be accepted and McNaughton appointed to the vacancy, but he was disposed to ask that the other two resignations should not be accepted, but be held up at least until Parliament was called and the matter brought before the House. The latter suggestion was apparently not discussed, but His Excellency agreed to take the required steps to change the Minister of National Defence if it should become necessary.

Several other preliminaries remained. King telephoned Mulock, a shaky conscriptionist, to ask him not to commit himself too far at the coming Council meeting but to wait and see what King had in mind. He agreed to do so. King also spoke to Claxton and apparently repeated his conversation with the Governor-General, for Claxton expressed his doubts on the ability of the Crown to refuse acceptance of a Minister's resignation. The Prime Minister next telephoned Crerar, a strong backer of Ralston, and suggested that he should not take a stand precipitately in Cabinet, for he had a new plan which he hoped Crerar would support. While Crerar's reply was non-committal, there was little danger after this conversation of his acting prematurely, which was all, presumably, that King hoped to accomplish. Finally, just before the Cabinet meeting, King had an interview with St. Laurent. He told him that General McNaughton was willing to take the portfolio and believed that he could raise the men without resorting to conscription. St. Laurent inquired what Ilsley and Macdonald would do under these circumstances, and King replied he had not seen them and thought it wiser to say nothing until the question came before the Council.

The Cabinet met shortly after three o'clock with eighteen members present.* Its tone was decidedly pessimistic, but the feeling was general that some definitive decision would have to be made before it adjourned. In the first two hours there was much re-threshing of old straw in a last endeavour to try to reach general agreement. Once again the question of picking up more volunteers was reviewed with a slightly more favourable report on the possibility of securing N.R.M.A. recruits. Once more the Prime Minister set forth his position on reinforcements, his continued belief in the voluntary system, his reluctance to call Parliament and especially to be responsible for a general election on the conscription question. Once more the Cabinet found itself searching for a formula for "necessary" conscription to which all mem-

*C. G. Power, C. D. Howe, and J. G. Gardiner were absent.

bers could give their approval. Finally, Ralston intimated that he might accept the compromise suggestion of an appeal for volunteers for a limited period with conscription to follow if the appeal was unsuccessful; but added that he would like that night to think it over. This was so at variance with his demand, reiterated time and again, that the question was urgent and that action must therefore be immediate that it aroused King's suspicions that some scheme might be afoot to place him in a position which he might find difficult to defend.*

From this point the story is best told in the Prime Minister's own words:

The moment I sensed this I felt the time had come for me to speak out. I kept waiting, expecting Ralston would repeat what he had said, that he would have to resign unless so and so were done. When I saw that, I felt that the situation would be worse tomorrow if I did not speak. I then said I thought we ought to,

---

*King recorded some hours later that at the time this proposal was made he did not think things out at all clearly, but that on reflection he was convinced that the conscriptionists were trying to narrow the dispute to so small an area that he could not easily refuse to accept the compromise. He also thought that there was the expectation that if he acquiesced, and "there was a failure to secure the necessary reinforcements I would not then allow a reference to Parliament." This last clause is difficult to comprehend, although it is quite intelligible if the words "be allowed" are substituted for "allow." The conscriptionist wing of the Cabinet did not want to have the matter referred to Parliament. Such action was not necessary under the Government's commitments until after the Order-in-Council enforcing overseas conscription had been passed; conscription might be defeated in the House; an election might result from active opposition in Parliament; and any submission of the issue would most certainly mean delay. At least one other Minister was uncertain what it was that Ralston wanted to consider further: the continued appeal, or the idea of a time limit, or the length of the trial period, etc. Ralston's speech in the House also sheds little light on the question. *Can. H. of C. Debates*, Nov. 29, 1944, pp. 6665–6.

if possible, reach a conclusion without further delay; that I had been told each day that an hour's delay would prejudice the securing of men; I did not see we would get any further by not getting an understanding at once. After what was said last night I realized that some way would have to be found, if it could be found, to save the government and to save a terrible division at this time, and at the same time make sure of getting reinforcements if that was possible at all. That I had been asking myself was there anyone who could do this; who believed that our policy, which had worked successfully for five years, would now work for the remaining weeks or months of the war. If there was, I thought it was owing to the country that such a person's services should be secured. I said I believed I had the man who could undertake that task and carry it out. I then mentioned Gen. McNaughton's name and said that there was no man in whom the troops overseas would feel their interests were being more taken care of than McNaughton. That there was no man toward whom the mothers and fathers throughout this country would have the same feeling more strongly; that there was no man in whom the citizens of Canada as a whole would have greater confidence for a task of the kind. McNaughton had taken no part in politics; was not a Liberal, a Conservative, or C.C.F., though he was very liberal-minded and very liberal in his policies. There was a difference between a campaign being started by a man who had little faith in what could be accomplished and by one who believed if he put his heart into it he could secure results. Ralston had said that while he was prepared to speak he did not think it would be of much effect. That I knew McNaughton felt otherwise; that he believed that tackled in the right way he himself could find the men necessary for reinforcements by the voluntary method. I then said I knew this because I had felt I must, as soon as possible, find someone who would undertake this task; that I should find out as soon as possible whether McNaughton would be willing to undertake it. I said I had talked with him this morning and I had an assurance from him that he thought he could get the reinforcements without resorting to conscription; that he thought conscription would be disastrous for Canada; that he knew the French-Canadians. Crerar had referred to the whole campaign centring on the hatred of French-Canadians, because of the so-called Zombie army and spoke about the whole situation being a flame across the country. I said McNaughton knew the French-Canadians and knew the prejudice that was being worked up. It would be a terrible thing for Canada if this was being permitted and if we had one province against the other. He was a strong believer in Canadian unity and believed the unity of Canada could be maintained, but not with conscription as an issue. That an attempt at this stage to do anything of the kind would have an appalling effect through years to come. I said that he believed he could get the reinforcements that were necessary. I pointed out that he believed our men were being given an undue share of fighting, being pressed too hard. . . .

I then said that the people of Canada would say that McNaughton was the right man for the task, and since Ralston had clearly said that he himself did not believe we could get the men without conscription, while McNaughton believed we could, and that he, Ralston, would have to tender his resignation, as he had said at different times he would do if we pressed eliminating the conscription part; that I thought if Ralston felt in that way, he should make it possible for us to bring in to the Cabinet at once—the man who was prepared to see this situation through. I said that in regard to a resignation from Ralston, that he had tendered his resignation to me some two years ago and had never withdrawn it; that that had been a very trying thing for me to go on day in and day out for this period with this resignation not withdrawn, but simply held. I then drew attention to the fact that no one could say that McNaughton was not the best person who could be secured. I drew from my pockets the exchange of letters, as printed, in September last, in which there is a statement that they have not seen eye to eye on some matters, but each shared the belief in the other's sincerity of conviction. I read the passage in which Ralston had made plain what McNaughton had done in training, etc.; his great skill, and certainty of his desire to serve Canada. I said there could be no misunderstanding as to McNaughton's qualifications.

I then pointed out that the hardest thing for any man to do was to part with a colleague, especially one who had been as close as Ralston had been, and of whom one had such high respect and, indeed, affection; but that these were times of war, the worst war the world had ever known. The situation particularly dangerous and that when it came to a government going under at this time, with all the consequences that that would produce in Canada and other parts of the world, I said I felt no man could allow satisfying his own conscience in carrying out what he had said to outweigh what his conscience must tell him would be the consequences for ill, of what he owed to the army and to the country and to the war effort. Ralston had taken up the words Canada's war effort as used by Crerar. He said that that was what he wanted to further. I pointed out that instead of furthering it it would destroy the total effort, destroy it in reference to finance and other things. I concluded by saying that I thought we ought not to allow this situation to drag on at all. The strongest of reasons had been given repeatedly why it should not, and that I thought we should decide at once what was to be done. There was intense silence.

Then Ralston spoke very quietly. He said that he would of course give me his resignation at once. He wished to thank me for the opportunity given him to serve. I had referred to having asked Ralston long ago to come into the Cabinet; that he had done [*sic*] great sacrifices. I had asked him before the war. He had said he could not, but if the war came, he would, and he did immediately. That I did not think any man had served the country more faithfully in every way or given the best of everything he had. Ralston went on to say that he had done the best he possibly could. He knew he was limited in some things, but had done his best. He spoke of the companionship we had enjoyed and what it meant to share in the work with his colleagues; that he sincerely hoped the new Minister—I forgot how he referred to him—I think he said the new move—might be successful. He was not sure that it would be but he certainly hoped it would. He ended by saying that he would retire to private life.

I replied that no words could express what we felt of his integrity, service, and the like; that it would be mere heroics to use any words regarding what we all knew so well. This was not a personal matter; it was what the situation at the moment seemed to demand. I thanked him for all he had done, and again expressed how hard it was for me to say what I felt I had to say in the interests of Canada's war effort.

Ralston then gathered up his papers and turned to me and shook hands. I have forgotten what he said. I think it was: he thanked me for the opportunity he had had. All the Cabinet rose, formed a complete circle around the table, and shook hands with him. As he was going out of the door I called to him that I wanted to have just a further word. I had spoken of the desirability of having the new appointment made at the same time as Ralston's resignation was accepted. I hoped that might be done this evening and have the matter cleared up today. At the door, I asked him whether it would be possible to let me have his resignation tonight. He had said he would write out his resignation. He looked very anxious and strained and said could he have until the morning. I said by all means but to please say nothing about it to any one; to keep the matter wholly secret and confidential, until the other appointment was made. This he said he would do.

I then went back to my seat and repeated to Council that it was one of the hardest things I had to do in my life, but that it was the only course I could see for me which would serve to meet the war situation. I then repeated that I felt every confidence that McNaughton would be able to get the reinforcements. . . . I mentioned he was not coming in in any political relationship or capacity but simply to do a job. This, when he felt it was a time of emergency and in the national interests to perform it if he were asked. There was again no comment at all.

I mentioned what I had said to Ralston about his resignation and said in Council I thought it would be better if we adjourned until eleven to-morrow morning. I swore the Council to absolute secrecy on what had been said. It was a scene I shall never forget, nor will those who were present.[30]

The following morning Ralston handed in his resignation, and McNaughton was sworn in as Minister of National Defence.

This concluded what was perhaps the most dramatic

incident in Canadian cabinet history. It speedily became one of the most controversial. Yet, viewed dispassionately, the part played by Mackenzie King—which was that most frequently attacked—is not open to serious criticism. The Cabinet was being torn apart over conscription, and there was no positive assurance at this time that the voluntary system might not yet produce the men required. A majority of the Cabinet were opposed to any change in policy, and no one knew where Parliament or the country stood on the issue. Even the conscriptionist Ministers did not want to use compulsion: they much preferred voluntary enlistment and were content, as it turned out, to give it one last opportunity to prove its adequacy. Few, if any, members of the Cabinet were disposed to blame Ralston for his determined stand, for they knew and appreciated his reasons; but by the same token it was most desirable, if the Cabinet were to show its complete sincerity in the continuance of voluntary recruiting, that he should relinquish his position. The Government by forcing the resignation of one of its ablest Ministers demonstrated in the most convincing fashion its determination to take every possible step to conciliate French Canada and to avoid conscription. That the war effort was to be maintained was attested by the appointment of McNaughton, whose devotion to the cause was not less than that of his predecessor. The Government had placed the emphasis on exactly the right spot: it desired no diminution in the prosecution of the war, but it was determined to continue under its existing policy of a volunteer system.

Thus while the Government could ill afford to lose a man of Ralston's inherent honesty and steadfast devotion, it could no longer afford to keep him unless it was willing to embrace conscription. That the Government was not prepared to do. It is one of the sure signs of an able Prime Minister that he will have the courage and toughness to get rid of men who have ceased to be an asset. Mr. Asquith once quoted with approval Gladstone's maxim that "the first essential for a Prime Minister is to be a good butcher" and then remarked: "there are several who must be pole-axed now." "Loyal as he [Asquith] was to his colleagues," added Mr. Winston Churchill, "he never shrank, when the time came and public need required it, from putting them aside—once and for all. Personal friendship might survive if it would. Political association was finished. But how else can States be governed?"* Mackenzie King possessed this ability to take harsh and extreme measures and he was prepared on occasion to sacrifice his associates for the sake of the larger purpose. Ralston, moreover, was not even the innocent victim Asquith had in mind, for he had many times announced in the Cabinet and

*W. S. Churchill, *Great Contemporaries* (London, 1937), p. 141. Franklin Roosevelt furnished a most interesting contrast, for he just could not bring himself to get rid of his assistants. In 1940 Harold Ickes knew that at least one member of the Cabinet (Woodring) ought to be removed, and he proposed to Roosevelt that he (Ickes) should make a statement at a Cabinet meeting on the desirability of the President reconstituting his Cabinet and suggesting that they should all resign and allow the President to rebuild his Cabinet as he wished. "The President seemed to appreciate my willingness to make a sacrifice hit, and after listening to me attentively, he said: 'But what would I say then, Harold?' My answer was that he shouldn't say anything, and he replied, 'Why, I couldn't do that, Harold. Some of the members of the Cabinet might think that I don't want them.' 'Well,' I retorted, 'there are some that you don't want, aren't there?' But he could not consent to my creating a situation that some members of the Cabinet might not understand as merely a plan to replace Woodring." Harold L. Ickes, "My Twelve Years with F.D.R.," *Saturday Evening Post*, June 5, 1948, pp. 90, 92.

Theodore Roosevelt was made of sterner stuff. "When he decided to cut a throat he generally justified it and rarely regretted it." William Allen White, *Autobiography* (New York, 1946), p. 451.

to the Prime Minister personally that unless conscription were adopted, he would have to resign. This was not the general vague kind of statement that if such-and-such a policy were followed he "would have to consider very carefully whether he would be able to continue as Minister," a carefully worded non-committal phrase with which every Prime Minister is only too familiar. Ralston had every intention of leaving, and King simply chose the most opportune moment for precipitating his departure.

It has, however, often been argued that the Prime Minister was unnecessarily abrupt and brutal in the manner of the dismissal, and the accusation contains a small particle of truth. But there are at least two circumstances which must not be overlooked in trying to make an honest appraisal. In the first place, the "brutality" was greatly exaggerated at the time by the hostile press and by Ralston's many friends. The essential facts have been stated above, and they will scarcely support the charge. The anti-Government press was eager to seize every pretext to discredit the administration, and the martyrdom of Ralston provided a welcome subject and evoked some extremely sympathetic passages which had been noticeably absent throughout the Minister's earlier career. The complaint of Ralston's friends is quite a different matter. They were sincerely moved by their own affection for him and were oppressed by a sense of injustice that so admirable a character should be summarily thrown aside in apparent disregard of his unselfish service. Had any one of several other members of the Cabinet been forced to resign under similar circumstances, it is certain that the keening over his departure would have been neither so loud nor so unrestrained.

Nor could the consciences of Ralston's many friends in the Cabinet be quite at rest, for they could not escape the uneasy feeling that by retaining their portfolios they had virtually given their *ex post facto* approval. Disturbed by a sense of guilt that they had allowed themselves to be the compliant accessories of a ruthless coup, and smarting with resentment against the Prime Minister for so deftly out-flanking their position, the conscriptionist Ministers were in no frame of mind to consider Ralston's dismissal dispassionately in the light of the public necessities of the case. It was hard for them to subordinate the claims of friendship to the imperatives of responsible government. They looked upon the dismissal as an act of unforgivable callousness, and, though their lips might be sealed by the vexing fact that they had not resigned with their friend and colleague but had remained members of a Government which rejected his advice, they could not be expected to stifle altogether a sense of outrage. Their feelings can scarcely have been soothed by the subsequent action of Mr. King in seating himself deliberately in the middle of the mourners' bench, as he did in uttering the following words a few weeks later in the House of Commons: "All of us revered our colleague the Minister of National Defence, and may I say that many of us, including myself, personally loved him."[31] Persuaded as they were of the hypocrisy of Mr. King's tears for the departed, it may fairly be surmised that the conscriptionist Ministers were prepared to hope that events would quickly justify Ralston's stand, and that in his vindication their own ambiguous position might be generously forgotten. Meanwhile they found some comfort in private recriminations against the greater guilt of the man whose hands had raised the pole-axe on high and brought it down on the head of their brother.

The second circumstance that must be borne in mind and one which largely and perhaps entirely justifies the manner in which the dismissal was accomplished was that King was confronted with the very difficult task of not only getting rid of Ralston but of retaining, if at all possible, the remaining members of the Cabinet. When George II asked Sir Robert Walpole how much it would cost to enclose Hyde Park, Walpole told him it would cost three Crowns. If Mackenzie King had not been extremely careful, his stand against conscription at this time would have cost him at least three Ministers, for Ralston, Ilsley, and Macdonald thought alike on the question. "I had to face the fact," said King in Parliament, "that if he [Ralston] were to leave the Cabinet, his resignation would probably be followed by the resignations of other Ministers. . . . The intimation was made very clearly that if Colonel Ralston went others would have to consider whether they would not have to go as well."[32]* King, as mentioned above, deemed it much safer not to discuss the availability of McNaughton with Ilsley or anyone else except St. Laurent. The plan which seemed most likely to succeed was to spring his decision quickly on the Cabinet and thereby make any resignations other than that of Ralston more difficult. Had the supporters of Ralston's proposal had any intimation of what was intended, they might well have united in a common action which would have brought down the government. The move, as it was actually carried out, caught everyone by surprise and made instantaneous concerted action almost impossible, and once that dangerous corner had been turned the situation became relatively safe. Every hour that passed thereafter stiffened the existing position. That evening Ralston persuaded Ilsley and Macdonald to stay and they, somewhat doubtfully, agreed to give

*The possible resignation of the three Ministers mentioned had been considered by King the day Ralston returned from overseas; Diary, Oct. 18, 1944.

McNaughton his opportunity: to resign then would give
little help to Ralston and would greatly injure the effectiveness of the war effort. King was, of course, unaware of their
attitude and was prepared the next morning to receive resignations from both Macdonald and Ilsley (he had in his mind
already chosen their successors); but he was reasonably
certain that they would not wish to come out against
McNaughton and his declared intention to make the voluntary system work. It was, therefore, the very unexpected
manner and occasion of the dismissal which made it successful, coupled with the fact that Ralston was the kind of
person who would place the good of the cause before any
thought of personal vindication. The only modification
which might have been justified would have been for King
to have summoned Ralston to his office immediately before
the Cabinet met, tell him of his intentions, and accompany
him directly to the Council chamber.

There must always remain some doubt whether Ralston
or King really wished to continue their association under
a situation involving substantial compromise on the major
question. Each had lost by this time any genuine desire to
work with the other, each felt that he could no longer rely
on receiving from the other the whole-hearted co-operation
and support which cabinet membership necessarily demands.
Any further association would have been at best an uneasy
companionship, equally distasteful to both: they disagreed
on a vital issue, and the severance of the relationship was the
only solution. Thus while Ralston in his letter of resignation
mentioned that the trial period for voluntary enlistment had
been considered, he insisted that the difference between the
Prime Minister and himself was "fundamental on the vital
matter of reinforcing our troops."[33] He later explained to
the House that the proposed compromise "was not the issue

on which I felt I had to leave the Cabinet. The basis of my resignation was the refusal to accept my recommendation [to invoke conscription]."[34] This was the transcendent question; and even had compromise been possible, Ralston would have been none too happy. He would not have obtained his reinforcements within the desired time, and he would always have remained sceptical of the genuineness of King's conversion and have been constantly on guard to detect the slightest signs of a relapse.

To the Prime Minister, Ralston was now so out of sympathy with Cabinet policy on conscription that it would be very difficult for Ralston to work whole-heartedly with some of his colleagues. King's contention that "there was a difference between a campaign being started by a man who had little faith in what could be accomplished and by one who believed . . . he could secure results" was true, and it was simply one manifestation of the unhappy situation. If King was determined not to have conscription if it was at all avoidable, he did not want a Minister at his elbow who was disposed to urge its adoption whenever the voluntary system or a limited conscription showed further signs of faltering. Hence his calm acceptance of the risk that both Ilsley and Macdonald might also leave the Cabinet. "I felt if it came to the worst," he wrote in his diary, "it would be a relief to be free of further conscriptionist elements in the Government,"[35] although their contact with conscription being more remote, he was not at all desirous of seeing them go. It is highly significant that at the very moment when Ralston showed signs that he might modify his position and might consider a middle course, King took alarm, and demanded that his resignation be submitted forthwith.

The dismissal of Ralston and the appointment of McNaughton must be regarded as an outstanding example of King's political shrewdness and his capacity for leadership which no consideration of the purely personal factors involved should be allowed to obscure. Events were soon to prove that McNaughton's appointment was no more than a stop-gap, but it enabled the voluntary system to be put to a final test and the experience of those few weeks convinced Quebec that it would have to accept the disagreeable alternative of compulsion. The only question then remaining was would Quebec prefer conscription to be applied by those who had been considerate of French-Canadian beliefs and feelings and had done their utmost to ward off the hated system, or would it prefer conscription to be applied by those who had reviled French Canada and had with vindictiveness advocated its enforcement. Resolved in these simple terms, the answer was simple also, and Quebec gave it.

THE *second* PHASE

The rumours and conjectures which for over two weeks had formed the nation's chief topics of discussion were dispelled in some measure by the change in the direction of the Department of National Defence. But the public still had little exact knowledge of the crisis or of the facts which had created it. It was known that the reinforcement situation was unsatisfactory and that the Cabinet deliberations had been primarily concerned with finding a remedy, and the replacement of Ralston by McNaughton indicated that there had been a Cabinet disagreement on policy which had been decided against overseas conscription and in favour of continuing the existing system. While the appointment of McNaughton was given at first a mild general approval, its reassuring effect was of brief duration. The conscriptionist and Opposition press lost little time in turning on their hero and denouncing him for agreeing "with the Government's cowardly and shameful policy of keeping the zombie army in futile idleness in Canada, and refusing to provide adequate reinforcements for the army he once commanded."[1] Even the newspapers which were normally favourable to the Government received the new Minister with reservations and were not disposed to do much better than suspend judgment for a time.[2] Ralston was known and trusted, and it was believed that in the nature of things he must be better informed than his successor whose recent contacts with the army had been slight. Quebec was the only area to receive the new appointment with enthusiasm, and it was greeted there as a "masterstroke." If McNaughton could ward off conscription when Ralston was apparently ready to throw in his hand, Quebec was ready to give its most fervent support to McNaughton. Mackenzie King, for his part, remained "the cavalier without fear and without reproach."[3]

Why did the new Minister believe that he could succeed where Ralston had failed? McNaughton, as already mentioned, was a sincere believer in voluntary enlistment, and the army which he had commanded and to which he gave unstinted devotion had been the product of this system. He believed that the reinforcement crisis was the product of faulty techniques and administration and that it should never have been allowed to arise. Fundamentally the trouble could be traced to bad planning: there had been undue delay in adjusting the reinforcements to the changes which had been made in the distribution of the troops overseas, and the result was an excessive supply in some arms and a deficiency in others. Moreover, the non-combatant personnel, both in Canada and in the United Kingdom, was unduly large, and the splitting of the Canadian forces between northwestern Europe and Italy had also made unusually heavy demands on men for communications and other supporting services. While it would clearly take time to overcome some of these difficulties and secure the transfer of the superfluous men, a good deal, he thought, could be accomplished at once with the

N.R.M.A. group, both by making their existing lot somewhat less attractive and by stressing and strengthening those factors which would induce them to enlist in the overseas army.[4]

These criticisms and suggestions, however, were not sufficient in themselves to justify McNaughton's confidence in his ability to revive the faltering voluntary system. It is evident that in weighing his problem he was also influenced to a material degree by his own feelings and emotions. His record indicated that he possessed conspicuous talent within certain fields, including a marked gift for leadership. His awareness of his ability, his striking appearance, and his attractive personality had produced great self-confidence, and this was in no way impaired by an ingrained optimism and a tremendous energy which led him to throw his heart into any project he undertook. He was stubborn up to a point, although he was able to make rapid readjustments in his thinking without, apparently, going through any intermediate stages, a kind of flexibility which usually proved most disconcerting to those associated with him. McNaughton's egotism had not been lessened by his career in the Second World War; his troops were devoted to him, and when he visited Canada in 1942 the public had given him the kind of welcome accorded a national figure of heroic proportions. His recall from the overseas command had left him with a smouldering grievance against Ralston, the Minister who had secured his retirement, and against General Stuart, who had succeeded him, while on the same count he had no cause to love some of the top British military officers. To become Minister of Defence would enable him to confound many of his critics, to discredit those who had discredited him only a few months before, and to occupy once again a position of authority and prestige. Nor could McNaughton with his keen sense of the dramatic be unmindful of the implications of his new appointment. His name, his reputation, his colourful personality might be counted upon to arouse the nation to a pitch of patriotic enthusiasm and bring the recruits to the colours, while at the same time the army —his army of volunteers—would be rescued from the menace and stigma of conscription. The man who had pointed "the dagger at the heart of Berlin" would now become the Cincinnatus called upon to save his country in its hour of need.

There is no suggestion here that McNaughton's belief in his policy was anything but genuine: these personal influences merely added to his confidence and made the flames of enthusiasm burn more ardently. Even so, he was prepared to admit that conscription might conceivably have to be used, though the circumstances of his appointment as Minister tended to obscure the fact that this reservation had been made. Thus when McNaughton first appeared in the Cabinet he stated clearly that he thought the reinforcements could be obtained on a voluntary basis, but added that if the need arose for resorting to extreme measures he would have to be assured that these were both necessary and appropriate. Speaking in the House some weeks later he said: "I contended . . . that we should make an honest and full endeavour to maintain our traditional system and to prove conclusively, to the satisfaction of ourselves and of all the country, that it could not be done, before we turned to measures which were more extreme."[5] Here, however, the emphasis had shifted, and it was caused, no doubt, by radical changes in circumstances which had occurred before the speech was made. Although the quotation might suggest it, McNaughton had never been a defeatist who expected to fail in his major effort: he was very sure that the men would respond, but he was willing at the same time to entertain the possibility that conscription might have to be used as a last resort.

The satisfaction which the Prime Minister derived from his success in meeting the Cabinet crisis proved to be short-lived, for the drive for volunteers under the new auspices encountered heavy going from the outset. General McNaughton's well-known enthusiasm, when put to the test, did not find expression in either prompt or inspiring action. Translated into the unfamiliar and uncongenial atmosphere of political conflict, he seemed unable to bring to bear on his immediate problem the energy which had hitherto been a striking personal characteristic. His initial inclination was to defer instituting any direct personal appeal until Armistice Day, an immediate loss of nine days which he could under the circumstances ill afford to sacrifice. At the prompting of the Prime Minister, however, he agreed to take earlier action. The occasions chosen were two meetings which had already been arranged for him, one at Arnprior on November 5 in support of the Victory Loan campaign, and the other at Ottawa a day later at a "Poppy Day" meeting of war veterans. At neither meeting was the response in any way encouraging, and his reception by the veterans in Ottawa was decidedly hostile. For one who liked to regard himself as a popular military hero it was a bitter experience to be cross-questioned, heckled, and contradicted by his own men and it was humiliating to find that instead of receiving enthusiastic support he was met by outspoken criticism tinged on occasion with cynicism and suspicion. The lustre of the General's personal popularity had already become somewhat tarnished by his entrance into politics. The soldiers believed he had let them down, and they were not disposed to transfer their confidence from Ralston to his successor without very good reasons.

On November 8 Mackenzie King, speaking on the radio, gave the nation the first official statement on the Cabinet crisis and the reinforcement situation. The speech was reassuring in tone and committed the Government to a continuance of the voluntary system, but it indicated that a redoubled effort would have to be made to keep the army up to strength. He appealed for more recruits, and added that there was a special obligation on the N.R.M.A. men to convert to overseas service.

Four days later Mr. Ralston, who had hitherto remained silent, gave his version of the crisis to the press, and the stock of the Prime Minister, which had enjoyed a modest rally, fell off once more. Ralston stressed the extreme urgency of the demand, pointed out that only the N.R.M.A. troops could make at once available a sufficient number of trained infantry, and disclosed for the first time that the "Government as a whole" did not consider that it was committed to overseas conscription for supplying reinforcements.[6] The impact of Ralston's statement on public opinion was little short of startling and it was speedily reflected in the attitude of the Liberal press which gave him increasing support. One immediate effect of the speech was to induce the Prime Minister to take steps on the following day to summon Parliament. He realized that either Ralston's statement would have to be answered at once or Parliament would have to be called to receive an explanation and to express its confidence or lack of confidence in the Government.[7] Ralston's statement had also increased the danger of other resignations from the Cabinet, for a substantial section of the press was now inquiring why some Ministers who apparently agreed with Ralston still remained among its members. King considered that the summoning of Parliament would at least postpone this danger, for if other Ministers should resign they could then not escape the obligation of defending their action in the House and especially their refusal to support voluntary enlistment under McNaughton's leadership. They would also be confronted with the immediate consequences of their act, involving, as it might, responsibility for bringing about the defeat of the Government.

The general attitude of the Cabinet during this troubled period was somewhat ambiguous: nominally united in its desire to make the voluntary system effective, it was nevertheless lukewarm in its efforts and in large measure somewhat sceptical of the result. Although not a single Minister was a conscriptionist by desire, a very influential group had become convinced of its inevitability, and these—the Ralstonites—were not quite sure what outcome they desired from the McNaughton campaign. They were sure that Ralston had been right, but there still might be a bare chance of McNaughton's making good, and it was therefore a chance worth trying. Yet, burningly conscious of the forced resignation of their colleague, they could not in their hearts wish his successor well, and they were not at all disposed to give him any substantial assistance or take their part in any "redoubled effort." Despite the very obvious fact that conscription had now more than ever become a national issue of the utmost consequence, they continued to regard it—and thereby justify their inaction—as a matter solely the concern of the Minister of National Defence and one for which they themselves bore little more than a nominal responsibility. Had this group been composed of the ordinary run of Ministers, this resentful aloofness might have made little difference. But it was not. It included a number of the ablest men in the Cabinet whose abstention tended to weaken the voluntary effort as much as their active support would almost certainly have helped to promote it.

Two other groups in the Cabinet were also plainly discernible. The French-speaking Ministers (except for La Flèche) were all anti-conscriptionists, but outside St. Laurent they carried very little weight, aside from that which flowed from their general position as the representatives of French Canada in the administration. A crusade aimed at encouraging enlistments from their compatriots might have yielded impressive results, but these Ministers were not the ones to make it: St. Laurent because he was still relatively untried politically and his gifts had hitherto appeared to lie in other directions, the remainder because they lacked both the ability and the prestige. The other outstanding anti-conscriptionist, C. G. Power, was in hospital during the greater part of this period, and his dislike of conscription was to some degree affected by a deep personal loyalty to Ralston. The third group was composed of Ministers who had always been followers rather than leaders, and they, true to their normal inclinations, were quite content to sit back and await the outcome of events.

At least three Ministers fell within none of these groups. C. D. Howe's interest in the conscription issue was for a long time one of indifference except when it threatened to interfere with the prosecution of the war. In the last days of the second phase of the crisis he became a conscriptionist. Brooke Claxton believed the existing system could be made to work if a vigorous plan of campaign were devised and carried out, and he was both able and energetic, but he had been in the Cabinet only a few weeks and his influence was naturally limited. Finally, there was the Prime Minister. He was naturally anxious to do what he could to assist McNaughton, but his capabilities in this direction were limited. He lacked the magnetism and the dramatic sense which would have enabled him to personify the Canadian community and its will to victory, and thus at this critical period supply dynamic leadership in a nation-wide campaign. At one time in his life, it is true, he might have rallied the country with rousing speeches which would break down the rational and emotional barriers erected by the N.R.M.A. troops, but those days were past. He was therefore well advised to confine his direct recruiting efforts to an appeal over the radio and to devote himself, behind the scenes, to the vital task of keeping the Government intact and thereby maintain the continuity and vigour of the Canadian war effort.

How far at odds the Cabinet were at this time and how unenviable was the lot of the Prime Minister in his effort to secure a measure of agreement were revealed in several statements given in private and in public by some of its members. Neither Macdonald nor Crerar, for example, was willing to allow Mackenzie King to forget for a moment that McNaughton's appointment was anything more than a respite and that as yet no substantial reinforcements were assured. In addition to raising the matter in Council, each addressed a series of letters to King in which they set forth what was essentially the same position. They desired that a specified limit should be placed on the recruiting period and that some assurance should be immediately given that if the effort failed to produce the men, the Prime Minister would then deem it "necessary" to pass the Order-in-Council which would send the N.R.M.A. troops overseas. Neither Minister was able to obtain from King the assurance he desired. Members of the Cabinet were not brought any closer together by a speech given by St. Laurent on November 5 at Quebec in which he expressed his complete confidence in the Prime Minister, urged greater tolerance and under-standing, and pointed out that had overseas conscription been applied at the time of Ralston's resignation "the majority of the Quebec population would have believed that it had been betrayed."[8] Nor, though in a quite different context, was Howe any more helpful when speaking at Chicago on November 15 he said that conscription in Canada was "rather a political question than a question of meeting an urgent need,"[9] or Ernest Bertrand who dismissed the agitation for conscription as "a fanatical explosion" designed to prevent the Liberals from carrying out their policies.[10] The effect of these provocative utterances on already troubled Ministers was not soothing, but the strain was somewhat relieved by the flamboyant pronouncement from General LaFlèche, the Minister of War Services: "When I found out that the situation was serious I asked the Prime Minister if I could go back to the front line. I offered as a guarantee of the good faith of my compatriots my life, my sword and my portfolio."[11]

This depressing ministerial atmosphere was little improved by the schemes which the Cabinet initiated to cope with the problem before it. A sub-committee was appointed on November 3 to consider General Service enlistments, and a report was submitted three days later. It made a number of suggestions designed to induce the N.R.M.A. men to volunteer and outlined a varied programme of radio addresses, individual approaches through the men's nearest relatives, co-operation by the clergy and the press, personal visits by General McNaughton to the N.R.M.A. camps in Western Canada, and other measures. A special report on French-Canadian infantry reinforcements was submitted on the same day by General LaFlèche. Another sub-committee of four Cabinet members was set up to create a civilian organization which would take over many of the functions recommended by the earlier committee. Despite all these preparatory measures and their approval by the Cabinet the great majority of the suggestions were never acted upon. A disbelief in their efficacy by some members, the reluctance of many Ministers to take an active part in pushing the proposals, an inability to work out and apply any comprehensive plan within the time available, all conspired to throw the burden of the recruiting effort back on the Department of National Defence.

Whatever the attitude of the Cabinet as a whole may have been there was no escaping the fact that the Minister of National Defence was charged with the primary responsibility for carrying out the Government's policy of recruitment, both because of his special ministerial relationship to the army and because of the nature of the circumstances under which he had taken office. McNaughton's top officers gave him little or no encouragement in his venture for they were quite convinced that the possibilities of the old system had been exhausted, but they naturally were bound to provide every assistance in a further trial. They warned him, however, that the time for experiment was limited to a few weeks, for if the reinforcements were to be used to fill up the pools they would have to leave Canada in December, and the shipping facilities had been arranged accordingly. It was evident, therefore, that only a vigorous recruiting campaign among the trained N.R.M.A. infantry, maintained at a high pitch for a short time, would be sufficient to meet the emergency.

But no such intense or exceptional effort could be discerned in the weeks which followed. General McNaughton in giving an account of his attempt to secure the reinforcements told the House of Commons that "since I took office [three weeks ago] I have pressed the application of the voluntary system by every means."[12] The story of this endeavour will not only throw some light on this statement, it is also essential to an understanding of the events which followed. General McNaughton's two speeches at Arnprior and Ottawa have already been noted: neither was addressed to the N.R.M.A. men, and in the first, this group was ignored. The Ottawa speech to the war veterans gave in outline the Government's policy towards the N.R.M.A. men, and if they read the newspapers carefully the message doubtless reached them in due course. These speeches began and ended McNaughton's efforts to make any direct approach —if this can be so described—to the group from which the great bulk of the reinforcements was to be drawn. If he was relying on the magic of his name and distinctive character to produce the recruits, he gave these presumably potent influences no chance to make themselves felt at close quarters. "You cannot do recruiting at long distance," commented Mr. Ralston, "either for general service or for N.R.M.A. men. It is like an evangelistic meeting; you have to have hand to hand work."[18] The only explanation which seems even remotely adequate is that the treatment McNaughton received at Arnprior and Ottawa proved so discouraging that he was not willing to risk coming to close grips with the intractable "Zombies" where his reception was likely to be even more rude and unrewarding. Whatever the cause, he addressed no more meetings; he visited no camps and showed himself to no N.R.M.A. soldiers; he studiously avoided making any appeal over the radio. He sat fast in Ottawa, and the great majority of the men he needed to reach remained in their quarters in British Columbia 2,500 miles away. Whatever special personal qualities General McNaughton may have hoped to bring to bear on the problem before him, he failed to put them to the test. Hurt and dismayed by the two minor encounters at Arnprior and Ottawa, he hastily drew back and made no further effort to win his victory by a direct frontal advance himself leading the assault.

This withdrawal deprived McNaughton of the use of his unique and most potent weapon, namely, his personality and his reputation in the mind of the common soldier. Henceforth he was compelled to resort to indirect methods by using the regular departmental machinery in his appeal for men, a method which Ralston had already discovered was insufficient. In leaving the recruiting effort in the hands of his district officers and others in charge of the N.R.M.A. troops, McNaughton had slipped into the old groove and thereby abandoned any hope of infusing any freshness or new vigour into the appeal for reinforcements. By the same token, he had in large measure placed himself at the mercy of a group of officers many of whom were by this time quite unsympathetic to the voluntary system.

On November 10 McNaughton sent out a general directive calling attention to the Prime Minister's recent broadcast and to his own two speeches, and urging that all officers in charge should use their best endeavours to raise men. This was the only attempt made by the Minister to reach these officers before November 14, twelve days after he had taken office. A very substantial part of the time available for his effort had therefore already elapsed.[14] On the 14th the general officers and district officers commanding and others met in Ottawa, and General McNaughton placed the problem before them, re-stated the Government's policy, and asked for their further assistance in carrying it out. The officers agreed to do their best, but held out no hopes whatever of obtaining the 15,000 men required by the end of December.*

*Before Ralston resigned he had received a report from his officers that an intensive recruiting campaign of three weeks would produce at the outside only 1,500 trained infantrymen. *Can. H. of C. Debates*, Nov. 29, 1944, p. 6673.

They stressed particularly the "hard core" of the N.R.M.A. men, those who had been exposed to intermittent recruiting efforts over a period of many months,* and had in the process built up strong defences against any further appeals along the same old lines. The officers were discouraged and their zeal for the voluntary system had evaporated; they felt they were pleading a lost cause to deaf troops; and it was clear that emotionally most of them preferred to see the appeal fail so that an adequate supply of men could be made easily available through conscription.

Although McNaughton was shocked at the strong conscriptionist feeling of these officers and the grim outlook for his policy which it implied, he refused to strike his flag. If the facts were unfavourable, he would try to ignore them and optimistically close his eyes to their ominous possibilities. He accordingly gave out the astounding statement in a press interview that "the information given me by the O.C.'s confirmed my belief more than ever that continuation of the voluntary policy will provide the reinforcements."[15] This was so utterly misleading that on November 19 four of the commanding officers who had been present at the meeting telegraphed their protests to McNaughton pointing out that they had told him the exact opposite and had said that they were quite sure that the intensified drive for recruits had no chance of success. McNaughton explained the incident to Mackenzie King in words which were meant to be reassuring; the diary reads:

The general explained that his confidence lay in the fact that while they [the officers] had spoken frankly of their doubts, they had nevertheless given the assurance they would make

*On September 30, 1944, out of 60,000 N.R.M.A. men enrolled, over 10 per cent had been there since 1941 and over 42 per cent since 1942.

another try and that he, himself, felt with that attitude and all
the forces that were at work and would now be coming to
work, for example, the individual efforts from men's families,
the Parliament meeting, public opinion shaping up, etc., etc.
that everything would come through all right.[16]

This is a most revealing account of the military mind
weighing political intangibles in the balances of an optimistic imagination. For if these were the most encouraging
forces that McNaughton could find coming to the aid of
his officers, the outlook was indeed hopeless. "The individual
efforts from men's families" were still part of a paper plan
which could get nowhere without an elaborate organization
that had not yet passed out of the embryo stage, which
would take many weeks to develop, and which in the end
might achieve very little. "The Parliament meeting," on
the other hand, was perhaps all too real a contingency; for
there was no assurance that Parliament would help the cause
of recruiting and its vote might well destroy the whole system. That "public opinion" was "shaping up" was true, but
unfortunately for McNaughton's scheme it was shaping up
in the wrong way, for it was daily becoming more and more
articulate in advocating the immediate despatch of N.R.M.A.
troops to Europe. One is perhaps justified in assuming that
the "etc., etc." (which may have come from McNaughton
or have been inserted by King) cover reasons which were
even less convincing than those stated in more specific terms.
Taken as a whole it was an extraordinary opinion to come
from the Minister who was most intimately concerned with
the problem, and it should have warned the Prime Minister
that this man liked to play with rosy fantasies which were
far removed from unpleasant realities. Yet there is no evidence that Mackenzie King tried to bring his Minister down
to earth. Realizing that the fate of the voluntary system

largely turned on the efforts of McNaughton, King may well have been anxious not to destroy his enthusiasm and thereby indirectly weaken the effectiveness of his effort. Moreover, King, too, wanted to believe "that everything would come through all right," and who could tell what the future might bring forth? Only ten days earlier King had pasted in his diary a cartoon bearing the inscription: "If you don't cross your bridges 'til you get to them; maybe they won't be there!"

The protest of the four commanding officers caused McNaughton to issue on November 20 a new press statement which was more accurately worded than its predecessor. It indicated that although the difficulties had been frankly stated by the officers, their "assurance of full support" had convinced the Minister that "the problem will be solved."[17] These words and the simple inferences to be drawn from them indicated that the Minister was beginning to appreciate the magnitude of his task and was inclined to gloss over the lack of confidence and sympathy displayed by his officers by dwelling on their promise of co-operation. No Minister should find it remarkable that government officials should be ready to support a Government's policy. McNaughton's officers were naturally bound to give him their honest and unreserved opinion on his proposals, no matter how disagreeable he might find it, but once he decided to go on with his policy, he should have been able, in fairness to the officers, to assume "full support." Is it at all conceivable that a Minister of Finance, who was about to open another Victory Loan or to continue a trade agreement, would ever dream of announcing to the press that he had every confidence that his problem would be solved, for although his civil servants had pointed out many difficulties they had also given him "assurance of full support" in implementing the Government's policy? To make a virtue of what was nothing more than a postulate of responsible government was an unmistakable indication of McNaughton's feeling of grave insecurity in dealing with his officers. They were not in sympathy with him or his renewed recruiting effort, and he was by no means sure that they would abide by the elementary rules of the game. Before the Minister issued the second press statement, he telephoned General Pearkes, one of the protesting generals,* read the proposed draft, and secured his approval.[18] While this was intended, no doubt, to be nothing more than an act of courtesy, it may well have been interpreted by officers in British Columbia as a further sign of the Minister's weakness and his desire to conciliate rather than fight back when opposed.

Immediate events certainly helped to confirm this interpretation. On General Pearkes's return from the D.O.C. meeting at Ottawa, he called the unit and command leaders together at Vancouver on November 20. Before the meeting opened these officers gave interviews to newspaper reporters in which they voiced their opinions on the Government's policy and the probable fate of a continued drive to secure conversions of N.R.M.A. men. These statements of five brigadiers and lieutenant colonels appeared in due course in the newspapers; short extracts from four of them are as follows: (*a*) The N.R.M.A. soldiers, announced Brigadier R. H. Beattie, "are just waiting the call from the Government that they must go, for they feel that it is the responsibility of the Government to implement its own legislation." (*b*) Brigadier G. A. McCarter said that he had studied the home defence situation carefully and discussed the problem with his commanding officers on many occasions, and as a result his opinion was that a campaign for volunteers would not succeed. The replies of the N.R.M.A. men when asked

*General G. R. Pearkes was at this time General Officer Commanding-in-Chief, Pacific Command.

to enlist, he added, "are always the same. They are waiting for the Government to give the order and they are ready to obey." (c) "Home defence soldiers," said Lieutenant Colonel J. MacGregor, "should not be expected at this stage of the game to make up their own minds. They are ready to go . . . but they are convinced the Government should tell them to go" (d) Lieutenant Colonel C. A. Scott also announced: "If the Government would only assume its responsibility, I am convinced this whole mess could be cleaned up."[19]

This endeavour to put pressure on the Government and ruin the recruiting effort was some years later excused by General Pearkes, himself an ardent conscriptionist, on the extraordinary ground that the interviews took place before the officers had attended his meeting and that they were therefore unaware of what the Government's policy was. Had the interviews occurred after the meeting, added the naïve General, the officers would naturally have remained silent.* Such an argument is scarcely worthy of a reply. The officers all knew the Government's policy perfectly well because it had never been changed. It had been restated by the Prime Minister and the Minister of National Defence two weeks before; it had been confirmed by the directive issued on November 10; McNaughton, following the meeting with the commanding officers in Ottawa, had issued his optimistic report on November 16. It was now November 20. The policy of the department had therefore been made unusually clear. The loquacious officers either did not know the duty they owed to the Government, or, knowing it full well, were determined to do what they could to influence public opinion on this most controversial subject.

General McNaughton, whether he was aware of it or

---

*Victoria *Colonist*, Oct. 23, 1952. This view is not the same as that expressed by General Pearkes on November 20, 1944. See *infra*, p. 88.

not, was thus again being put to the test. The army was once more taking the Minister's measure, reasonably certain that it could oppose his policy with impunity. Had McNaughton had more confidence in himself and in his ability to cope with the situation, he would have eagerly welcomed the occasion, so opportunely presented by a few brigadiers and lieutenant colonels, to meet head on this challenge to the supremacy of the civil power, while at the same time he could have shown the whole army that he meant his renewed recruiting campaign to be taken seriously. But he dodged the issue, and thereby confirmed the officers' opinion that the Minister lacked both courage and decision. His quite inadequate reply was to appoint General Sansom to investigate the incident and make a report. This report was presented a few weeks later, and it completely exonerated the officers on the charge of infringing army regulations.[20] The only thing which was lacking was a citation for conspicuous loyalty or a special medal for so courageous a denunciation of official policy.

The first three weeks of November witnessed a decided swing in public opinion on recruiting policy. The alarming reports from overseas, Ralston's hurried trip, the prolonged Cabinet discussions, the change of Ministers at National Defence, the realization that existing recruiting procedures were failing to produce enough men, each of these exerted its pressure in the same general direction. While the issue had become a party question so far as the official Opposition could make it so, it tended to cut across party lines to an increasing extent as time went on. French-speaking Canada, exemplified by Quebec, was still anti-conscription to a man, and there were undoubtedly many others throughout the Dominion who sincerely believed that compulsion would do far more harm than good. All these were obviously in favour of continuing the voluntary system. At the other extreme were the conscriptionists who were equally convinced that the time was long overdue for putting their plan into effect. In between were a very large and indeterminate number whose views might be identified in a general way with those of Ralston and his supporters in the Cabinet. These were fast taking up a position where they were unwilling to make any further concessions to conciliate the French and where they were prepared to enforce conscription regardless of its consequences in Quebec. Once they had reached this point, reason tended to fall into the background and their emotions swept them on. They were inclined to over-estimate the seriousness of the emergency, the number of reinforcements needed, the urgency for their dispatch, the perilous position of the men at the front, the fighting qualities of the N.R.M.A. men, the reluctance of the French to enlist, the probable length of the war, etc. The longer they dwelt on these matters the more their resolution hardened and the more they tended to regard any continuance of the voluntary system as futile and irritating, an intolerable impediment to the winning of the war. A summary, prepared by the Wartime Information Board, dated November 20, said:

The majority of reports from English-speaking areas, though reflecting some lessening of emotional tension, are still firmly in favour of immediate conscription. The controversy has clearly aroused a genuine anxiety about reinforcements, and people are talking a good deal about the long periods spent in the front line and about men recently transferred to the infantry who have become casualties. Observers also stress the demand for 'equality of sacrifice,' the talk about 'appeasement of Quebec,' the fear of open conflict between returned soldiers and N.R.M.A. men. . . . The superiority of a volunteer army is said to be sharply questioned, and the plea for 'national unity' rejected on the ground that it does not exist now. A minority of observers report some opposition to conscription on the grounds that it would disrupt the country. . . .

The newspapers naturally played a prominent part in this discussion, and most of the metropolitan papers carried at least one editorial a day dealing with some phase of the reinforcement situation. Virtually all the French-language press was opposed to conscription on principle. English-language papers were divided between those which wanted conscription immediately and accused the Government of trying to appease Quebec by avoiding the issue, and those which believed the Government would introduce conscription when necessary. The first group comprised papers which generally supported the Conservative party, the second was made up of regular supporters of the Liberals. By mid-November, however, the Liberal papers were fast becoming converted to the Ralston position.[21]

The tactics of the Progressive-Conservative party and press were fairly simple. Mackenzie King had said that if the voluntary system failed, Canada would have conscription, and the Conservatives therefore set about to make the policy fail, thereby vindicate their endorsement of conscription, and force the sons of Quebec overseas. Few Conservatives were converts to conscription of more than two years' standing,* but that in no way lessened their dogmatism or mitigated the bitterness of their advocacy. Throughout November their outcries had become increasingly shrill as the acknowledged shortages in reinforcements gave support to an anti-Government campaign which for years had been rendered ineffective by an evident lack of grounds for criticism. The crisis in the Cabinet gave the signal for an outpouring of unscrupulous propaganda such as Canada had not seen for at least a generation. No opportunity was lost to depreciate the Government's conduct of the war, to give full publicity to any soldier's grievance, to exaggerate

*Mr. Bracken did not declare himself unequivocally for conscription until November 1944. Winnipeg *Free Press*, Nov. 11, 1944.

the consequences of the shortage of men, and to harrow the public's feelings with stories of the soldiers fighting at the front while the Cabinet "played politics" at Ottawa. Rumours were given credence, proclaimed, elaborated, and discussed as though they were the truth. The wrath of the Conservative party and its press was turned especially on Quebec, and attacks on the voluntary system became in large measure attacks on that province and the manner in which it had failed in its duty. The number of men from Quebec who had enlisted and were in the N.R.M.A. camps was compared with those from other provinces,* and it was asserted that the only reason that the Liberal Government did not favour conscription was because so large a part of its parliamentary following came from French Canada. "The Government," wrote one Toronto paper in a typical passage, "is wickedly sacrificing young men's lives to retain its governing power in Quebec."[22] The hatred of the Liberal party, the determination that the young French Canadians should be made to fight, and the desire to support the army in Europe seem to have inspired these outbursts in approximately equal proportions. This disreputable page in Canadian history was summarized at the time by Senator J. J. Bench:

I blame a section of the press, who by every device in the editorial repertoire—news columns, cartoons, front-page features, anonymous letters from our troops, and printed opinions—have played upon the affections and anxieties of Canadian citizens until they reached a breaking point. This was no spontaneous

---

*Total percentage of enlistments in relation to estimated male population, ages 18 to 45, up to September 30, 1944, was 23.4 per cent in Quebec and 40.3 per cent to 47.1 per cent in other provinces. National average was 38.6 per cent. Wartime Information Board, *Canada at War*, No. 44 (Feb.–March 1945), pp. 52–3. On November 8, 1944, there were in the N.R.M.A. camps about 60,000 men, of whom 23,000 were from Quebec. W.L.M.K., Radio Address, Nov. 8, 1944.

outburst . . . here was a studied propaganda carried on over a period of many months . . . even before our troops were in action.*

General McNaughton did not escape. The malignity of Conservative partisanship turned also on the man the party had wanted for its leader and he was accused of betraying the army. An amusing example of the pettiness of the agitation against him was his demotion in some quarters to "Mr." McNaughton as soon as he entered the Cabinet, while Colonel Ralston, the transient hero of the Opposition, was allowed to retain his rank, presumably to emphasize his special knowledge of military affairs. McNaughton was also represented as knowing little about the war: he "speaks from hearsay. He has never been to the firing line in this war. He has been away from the army since December 27 last."[23] After a few days of office and after receiving a deluge of letters of protest and abuse McNaughton remarked that he thought he was now the most hated man in Canada. The Prime Minister's reply was no doubt all too true: "I still thought I could do him one better on that score."[24]

General McNaughton might fairly assert, and he did assert it later in Parliament,[25] that the Government's endeavour to raise the reinforcements was frustrated by a lack of public support. While this does not furnish a complete explanation, there can be no doubt that the newspaper campaign and the swing in public opinion worked powerfully to discourage recruiting, with the Minister doing nothing whatever to counteract the trend. Uncertainty was fatal. The more doubtful the outlook for the voluntary system and the more imminent the prospect of conscription, the greater was

*Toronto *Globe and Mail*, Dec. 6, 1944 (edit.). The newspaper commented: "The cap fits and *The Globe and Mail* will wear it. This newspaper is not embarrassed by anything it has done to bring the facts of the tragic two-army policy to the people."

the inducement for the men to refuse to volunteer and to hold back and await future action.

It was therefore not surprising that the reinforcement situation during the first three weeks of November was disappointing. The handicaps were apparently proving too heavy to be overcome. The Cabinet was far from being effectively behind the recruiting drive; the army was giving it only a moderate degree of support; the efforts of the Minister of Defence, despite an unquenchable optimism, were scarcely perceptible, nor did they appear to receive any special impetus from the office of the Prime Minister; newspaper criticism was becoming more pronounced; and public opinion outside Quebec was showing an increasing exasperation at the delay in dispatching the much needed infantry. There was, of course, some progress. McNaughton was able to report that two or three thousand General Service men had been shaken loose from the masses stationed in Canada and the United Kingdom, but some of these at least had been anticipated before he took office. The new enlistments and the conversion of N.R.M.A. men showed small gains,* but here also the numbers were lamentably inadequate. How-

*The figures were:

	General Enlistment	N.R.M.A. Conversion	Total
Nov. 1–7	962	160	1122
Nov. 8–14	923	186	1109
Nov. 15–21	1047	348	1395
Total	2932	694	3626

The above figures were later revised by the army, but these were the ones actually used at the time. The N.R.M.A. conversions, the vital soldiers for immediate reinforcement, were for the above three weeks only slightly more than one-half of those for the whole month of August (1,350) and September (1,340), though slightly above the monthly *rate* for October (848). *Can. H. of C. Debates*, Nov. 23, 1944, p. 6545.

ever, by November 13 McNaughton reported that he had
sufficient troops available to fill all his transports up to the
end of December, although many thousands were still
needed to make good the deficiencies in the reinforcement
pools. Mackenzie King, wishing to see the effort succeed
and encouraged by the optimistic reports of his Minister of
Defence, was still disposed to be cheerful, but one of his
more realistic Ministers had a better grasp of the situation
when he wrote on November 14: "It now looks as though
this appeal would not succeed any better than the other."
Once more uncertainty and restlessness returned to haunt
the Cabinet meetings as the Ministers found themselves
back in the old quandary—for conscription or against? how
many Ministers on one side, how many on the other? how
keep the voluntary system and not lose the conscriptionists
or how adopt conscription without forcing out the Ministers
who considered they were bound to oppose it? A definite
decision could not be much longer delayed, for the meeting
of Parliament on November 22 set a rigid deadline and the
Cabinet obviously could not face the Commons divided and
without a policy.

The ineluctable approach of the second phase of the
conscription crisis found the Prime Minister in a state of
uncertainty and misgiving little better than that of three
weeks before. His hopes for a successful issue in voluntary
enlistment, while not abandoned, were weakening; he shrank
from imposing conscription under the existing circumstances,
and yet he realized that somehow substantial reinforcements
had to be provided. He was still seeking a compromise which
would hold the Cabinet together, although he had by
now come to regard the loss of some Ministers as probably
inevitable, no matter what the final solution might be.
Characteristically he was determined to put off the *dénoue-*

ment as long as he possibly could, for the postponement not only left an opportunity for settlement at the last moment but also gave him more time to allow his own ideas to take shape.

The day before Parliament was to meet King's line of action had become fairly clear though it could scarcely be said to be at all rigid. It was the product of three major objectives: to maintain national and party unity; to obtain the necessary reinforcements; and to avoid compulsion— these being stated in the order of importance which King attached to them. He presented his case to the Cabinet in his most conciliatory fashion:

I told the Cabinet I had been thinking matters over very carefully. Realized there was a difference which apparently was irreconcilable. Both sides equally sincere in their position. That I wanted to keep the party united for its service to Canada and to the world at this time. I recognized there was a voluntary enlistment wing and a conscriptionist wing. That, except in that, we did [not] differ. The difference would go when the war was over. In the meantime we must try and not let bitterness make the cleavage too wide so that we could come back naturally together later on. I thought that we were all agreed the appeal should be continued for a certain length of time. Definite time should be fixed when appeal should end, and if at that time we had not the adequate number of men I would then make it possible for conscription to be enforced without going back to Parliament for any vote of confidence. That I would myself resign and ask H[is] E[xcellency] to call on some one member of the Cabinet to form a Government to carry through conscription. I then told Council of my determination not to have dissolution in war time and made some mention of the other thoughts I had in the morning.* When I spoke of my own

---

*Chiefly this: "I shall not take any step which will prevent the men who are fighting overseas from obtaining needed reinforcements by any method that is feasible. I have taken the only method I believe possible. It is for those who believe in a different method to be given the opportunity of carrying it out." Diary, Nov. 21, 1944.

intention to drop [out] and let those who believed in conscription carry on, there was a period of intense silence in the
Cabinet. No one said a word. All were silent so long that I
myself had to break the silence by an observation or two.²⁶

These words reveal that the Prime Minister fully realized
that the ring was closing fast about him. The past few weeks
had yielded pitifully inadequate returns and the attitude
of conscriptionist Ministers was turning from impatience
to rigidity. There was, moreover, no reason to believe that
the anti-conscriptionists would be willing under any circumstances to modify their position. King's offer, stated above,
was a desperate attempt to intervene in time to prevent
either side from assuming a position on which the Government might break up. He sought to reassure the anti-conscriptionists by the offer of a further trial period and at the
same time he met the conscriptionists half-way by his admission that failure must be followed by a complete surrender.
In the latter event, he himself would resign. This was not as
self-effacing, perhaps, as it appeared on the surface. The
prospect of resignation by the Prime Minister was a two-
edged sword which could be turned against both extremes.
It would spell disaster to the anti-conscriptionist Ministers and
the maintenance of the voluntary system, since King's abdi-
cation would remove their leading protagonist; it would also
compel the conscriptionists in the Cabinet to face the disagreeable alternative of having to seek support from their
traditional party foes and delay for many weeks the achievement of their main end.

These possibilities were all implicit in King's statement
to the Cabinet. Most of the Ministers immediately responded by declaring that they would stand by King, and were
prepared, if necessary, to resign with him. The conscriptionist remainder, especially Crerar, Ilsley, and Macdonald,
had been very outspoken in Council the day before the above

appeal was made, and had indicated then that they were decidedly averse to any lengthy postponement of the passage of the necessary Order-in-Council. Although they were still not prepared to take a final stand against another trial period, enough was said at the later meeting to show that they regarded immediate resignation as their inevitable course. Sensing that these Ministers were fast approaching a final break, King made a special plea to Ilsley, pointing out how vital his services were and how, if the members in the War Committee were to withdraw their support, he as Prime Minister did not think that he could take on the extra responsibility which that withdrawal would entail. Ilsley's position was crucial. He occupied the same pivotal position among the English-speaking members as did St. Laurent among the French. His ability, industry, and character were outstanding, and everyone recognized his exceptional conscientiousness and his fearless advocacy of what he considered to be the right. His close friendship and sympathy with his fellow Nova Scotians, Ralston and Macdonald, would make his decision carry an additional weight. King, in wording his appeal in these terms, was turning to advantage his knowledge of Ilsley's deep sense of responsibility and his ingrained aversion to the making of any hasty or ill-considered decision. The effort met with at least partial success in that Ilsley withheld expression of any final commitment at this particular time.

Nevertheless, a settlement of the issue could not long be deferred. The Cabinet had reached the point where it had to break or secure a major sacrifice of principle from one side or the other. Despite the fact that the anti-conscriptionists were in a numerical superiority in the Cabinet, they held by far the weaker cards. For if the French-Canadian Ministers and those who sympathized with them resigned, the

Government fell, and the remainder united with the minority parties to put conscription into effect. If the conscriptionists resigned, again the Government fell, and again the new Cabinet would be composed of a coalition of conscriptionists of all parties. Resignation by either section of the Cabinet could therefore bring only defeat to the anti-conscription cause.

All these potential discords were scarcely veiled by the terms of a resolution which the Cabinet unanimously accepted for submission to the House on the following day, namely, that "this House will aid the Government in its policy of maintaining a vigorous war effort." Later in the day King "talked over with St. Laurent the appalling situation that I was being placed in of thinking of carrying on the Government without Ministers like Ilsley, Howe and practically all the Ontario Ministers. . . . I cannot see how I could carry on without Ilsley and Howe in particular."[27] He looked forward to the morrow, however, with no despondency, but a mild pessimism: the parliamentary session, the party caucus, the general uncertainty, the possible resignations were "all going to be extremely difficult and trying." But he went to bed undismayed and enjoyed an untroubled night's rest.*

On the morning of November 22 King was about to make his preparations for the opening of the House when he was called to the telephone. It was General McNaughton.

He said he had quite serious news. That the Headquarters Staff here had all advised him that the voluntary system would not get the men. He had emphasized it was the most serious

---

*Mackenzie King's ability to get a good night's sleep was astonishing. From the time of Ralston's return (Oct. 18) to November 30 he recorded three restless nights (Oct. 19, 31, Nov. 25) and only one (Nov. 20) in which he really slept very little.

advice that could be tendered and he wished to have it in writing. Said he would come and see me as soon as he had the written statement. He expressed the opinion that it was like a blow in the stomach. He also said that he had the resignation of the Commander in Winnipeg. That if the Commanders, one after the other, began to resign, the whole military machine would run down, begin to disintegrate and there would be no controlling the situation.

Instantly there came to my mind the statement I had made to Parliament in June as to the action the Government would necessarily take if we were agreed that the time had come when conscription was necessary. It is apparent to me that to whatever bad management this may have been due, we are faced with a real situation which has to be met and now there is no longer thought as to the nature [accuracy?] of the military advice tendered, particularly by Gen. McNaughton. And if so tendered by Gen. McNaughton who has come into the government to try to save the situation, it will be my clear duty to agree to the passing of the Order in Council and go to Parliament and ask for a vote of confidence, instead of putting before the House the motion that I have drafted and intended to hand the clerk. This really lifts an enormous burden from my mind as after yesterday's Council it was apparent to me that it was only a matter of days before there would be no Government in Canada and this in the middle of war with our men giving their lives at the front. A situation of civil war in Canada would be more likely to arise than would even be the case were we to attempt not to enforce conscription. As I look at the clock from where I am standing as I dictate this sentence, the hands are both together at 5 to 11.[28]

The decision to make the transition from the voluntary system to conscription thus took only a few minutes and it was completed in the Prime Minister's mind before eleven o'clock that morning. To many people it was an inexplicable and illogical change, but some knowledge of the background and the events of the past month or so should dispel at least in part the mystery which has been attached to the making of the fateful decision.

The immediate cause of the *volte-face* was obviously the memorandum presented by the Chief of the General Staff on behalf of the Military Members of the Army Council* on the morning of November 22 that "every effort within our power has been made to meet this problem [of reinforcements] by the voluntary system. After a careful review of all the factors including the latest expression of their views by the District Officers Commanding, I must now advise you that in my considered opinion the Voluntary system of recruiting through Army channels cannot meet the immediate problem." To this announcement must be added General McNaughton's opinion given to King that the Government's policy was not receiving the support from the army to which it was entitled, and King's own concern over his disintegrating Cabinet. The action on November 22, however, does not stand alone: it must be regarded in the light of what had gone before and according to the interpretation which McNaughton and King placed on a number of these events.

General McNaughton had been in office only a short time when he began to entertain doubts and apprehensions about the loyalty of his subordinates. He was extremely conscious of the fact that very few of his officers were in sympathy with his endeavour to make the voluntary system work. He had their nominal support and in many instances their complete co-operation, but most of them were against him by

*The Army Council was a wartime body, the personnel of which changed slightly from time to time. In 1944 it was composed of the Minister of National Defence, the two civilian deputy ministers and five officers of high rank: the Chief of the General Staff, the Vice-Chief of the General Staff, the Adjutant-General, the Quartermaster-General, and the Master-General of the Ordnance. The five officers were commonly referred to as the Military Members. Following the order given above, these officers were respectively Lt. Gen. J. C. Murchie, Maj. Gen. R. B. Gibson, Maj. Gen. A. E. Walford, Maj. Gen. H. A. Young, and Maj. Gen. J. V. Young.

conviction. There had been far too much said about the officers who, despite their beliefs, "loyally undertook to make another effort," as though they deserved great credit for discharging their evident and inescapable duty. No Minister, even if he had not been a former commander of an army, would feel particularly honoured at receiving this kind of condescending co-operation, and McNaughton was more sensitive than most. He developed misgivings and suspicions and was constantly on the alert for signs of disloyalty and resentment. These he passed on to the Prime Minister, partly because he believed them, and partly, no doubt, because they helped to excuse and divert attention from his own inadequacy in securing recruits.

On November 13, for example, General McNaughton confided to King that although the army had been built up as a voluntary organization, there were some who were "plotting" to secure conscription. There was also a potential danger, he thought, from another quarter if ever the Government should introduce conscription. In such an event, most of the soldiers who would have to maintain law and order and compel N.R.M.A. men to go overseas would themselves be drawn from the N.R.M.A. ranks.* Bloodshed would be likely to occur, and the enforcement troops might well be found on the wrong side. Some days later McNaughton anticipated more trouble with the senior officers who had questioned the accuracy of his statement to the press concerning the meeting of the D.O.C.'s.† "He said to me," wrote King, "that he had to handle these men very carefully. That if he began to oppose them, he might have a revolt on his hands and a situation which would be very

---

*This is a curious argument, for it apparently disregards the 120,000 General Service men serving in Canada.
†*Supra*, p. 68.

difficult to manage. The one thing to do was to avoid any quarrel; to explain quite clearly what he meant and express the hope that they would, with that understanding, do their best to further the new policy." Again on November 20 McNaughton confided to King that "he felt there was a real conspiracy right in the department itself, not to have this voluntary system work. If given a fair chance he believes it would succeed, but instead of helping, everything possible was being done from different sources to enforce conscription. . . . He was fully convinced that the policy would work if given a chance." That King was influenced by these talks is attested by the comment in his diary on the press interviews given by the officers in British Columbia: "It is quite apparent that there is a conspiracy there. One after the other has been coming out and saying that the N.R.M.A. men were just waiting for the Government to do its duty and send them overseas. That looks like the Army defying the civil power. These men in uniform have no right to speak in ways which will turn the people against the civil power."[29]

But McNaughton's views were based on more than fears and surmises, for he had some concrete evidence to give them at least a partial confirmation. The attitude of many officers was known to be openly hostile to further recruiting efforts, and there had been some talk, which may well have come to McNaughton's attention, that a number of them were considering the advisability of resignation as a means of putting pressure on the Government to pass the desired Order-in-Council. The protest of the four senior officers on November 19 was in itself not alarming, but occurring at that time on that subject it could well be considered both provocative and disturbing. No one, moreover, could ignore the significance of the press interviews given by the officers in British Columbia, and these had been encouraged by

General Pearkes, in charge of the Pacific Command, who produced for the occasion a new kind of military obligation. "Before the Conference opened, Gen. Pearkes told the assembled officers that they had a duty to the public to inform it of the situation. He declared he had no objection to the officers stating their ideas of the reaction of the N.R.M.A. recruits to the appeals of the Prime Minister and the Minister of National Defence."[30] Finally, there was the resignation of Brigadier R. A. Macfarlane as Officer Commanding Military District No. 10 (Winnipeg), which occurred only two days later as a protest against the recruiting plans of the Government. He declared that 99 per cent of the officers in Canada favoured conscription, and that he resigned because he could not conscientiously do his job as a soldier under the existing system of raising reinforcements.[31]

The attitude of some of the military authorities is further brought out by the timing of the presentation of the memorandum by the Military Members of the Army Council. Its avowed purpose was simply to inform the Minister that the Military Members considered that the voluntary system could not produce the men and that they felt that they could not take the responsibility for advising its continuance. Why did they submit the memorandum on the morning of the day that Parliament met? To assume that this was a mere coincidence would be straining credulity too far. Why did the time-limit which the Military Members had given their Minister run out on this particular day? They had said "a few" weeks, which would mean three weeks as the absolute minimum. They gave him in fact only twenty days. Moreover, while the recruiting remained at a low figure, this and other methods had produced some thousands of men, so that McNaughton had been able to inform King on November 13 that he then had enough troops available to fill his transports up to the end of the year. Any dead-line, therefore, which was based on transportation facilities as contemplated when McNaughton took office on November 2 could have been postponed as a result of the change in this vital factor. Yet this was not done. The army officers were surely pressing their Minister very hard when in view of the above lessening in transport pressure* they abruptly terminated his trial period one day before the minimum given him under more unfavourable circumstances. It is also certain that this ultimatum—so regarded by McNaughton, whatever its form —was quite unexpected, for he had been saying in Cabinet only two days earlier that another fortnight's experience would enable them to form a better judgment on how the appeal was progressing. What was the special urgency on November 22 if it was not the meeting of Parliament, and what the purpose except to apply pressure to the Government?

Further examination, moreover, reveals that the date is not consonant with the timing of other events which are related to it. The conference with the officers commanding had taken place in Ottawa on November 14, and the British Columbia meeting which was to launch the invigorated recruiting drive in that province was held on November 20. How did the Military Members of the Army Council expect to see results from a campaign which in the major camps had lasted less than two days? Why allow this drive to get started at all knowing as they must have known, that it would not have any chance to yield results before they would foreclose on the Minister for lack of time?

The Military Members would no doubt have supplied one

*This was supported later by the facts, for the first drafted N.R.M.A. men did not sail from Halifax until January 3, 1945. C. P. Stacey, *The Canadian Army, 1939–1945*, p. 235. Additional transports, however, could frequently be obtained from New York, although apparently they were not available on this occasion. *Can. H. of C. Debates*, Nov. 23, 1944, pp. 6527, 6548.

answer to all these questions and criticisms. The Minister had done nothing during his tenure of office which would hold out any promise that enlistment on a large scale was even a remote possibility. On the contrary, he had demonstrated by his failure to try anything new and his willingness to fall back on the old and now inadequate methods that he had no helpful contribution to bring to the solution of the problem. An allotment of twenty days for the national campaign and of two days for that in British Columbia was indeed meagre and insufficient; but the officers saw no reason to believe that more time would work any substantial change. "Nothing was being *done*," exclaimed one of them some years later. "Nothing was *happening*. We were just wasting precious time and getting nowhere!" This is a plausible explanation of why the Military Members moved as they did, and it acquits them of any charge of unworthy motives. But it cannot excuse such direct action against their Minister. The Government wanted the effort made along the lines it had determined, and the Military Members were not justified in trying by an implied threat to impose their will on their Minister on the very day that Parliament assembled.

There has been a good deal of talk—originating in some measure at least with Mackenzie King[32]—about a possible military revolt in Canada at this time. So far as can be ascertained the only evidence is that given above. There was a lack of enthusiasm and a lack of effort in the cause of voluntary enlistment among the army officers who in many instances placed personal convictions and feelings above the legitimate demands of the Government; there was apathy and a disinclination to help in some quarters which may have approached a mild form of passive resistance; there was the conviction in the minds of many army officers that the civil power was not doing its duty and that therefore the army was free to do as little as it pleased to assist; there was a withdrawal of support by the Military Members of the Army Council for the Minister's policy; but there is no sign whatever of ardent soldiers in a spirit of misguided patriotism being prepared to march on Ottawa and take over the government.

The presentation of the memorandum by the Military Members was, in fact, considered to be a venturesome move by its authors. While there was no explicit agreement among them that they would resign if their advice were not followed, at least one or two of them understood that in the event of the Minister remaining adamant, resignation would be the next step. They were all aware that the Minister or the Cabinet might call them to a swift account, but in view of McNaughton's conciliatory attitude when opposed by the army, this risk would seem to have been very small. The story is told that on the evening following the presentation of the memorandum, the Military Members sat around headquarters awaiting possible execution. At last, as midnight approached, one of the more philosophic generals rose and said: "I'm going home: if they want to fire me, they can fire me just as well in bed."

General McNaughton's response to the memorandum should have been to fight back against the improper and premature pressure which his top officers were exerting against him. Would it not have been reasonable for him to have insisted on another two weeks to demonstrate beyond any doubt that the voluntary system had failed—or succeeded? The fact that McNaughton changed his policy so quickly and with so little protest meant he was convinced that it had failed; it also meant that he was aware of the feeling against him and his inability to stand up against his officers. It is very likely that the Military Members of the Army Council would have resigned if the Government had persisted with voluntary enlistment and had rejected their implied recommendation of conscription. The defeat of the Government might have followed. On the other hand, McNaughton might have demanded that these dissenting members of his Council should retire in a body to be replaced by others more sympathetic to his purpose. But where was he to find successors, and, even if he were able to do so, was he so certain of his support in the army that such a drastic shake-up would not have been met with a flood of resignations across the Dominion? These were by no means improbable contingencies. Thus while it is true that there was no revolt in the Canadian army, there was a real trial of strength between the civil and the military powers. There is no doubt that the soldiers were playing with political gunpowder and the consequences could have been catastrophic if a few matches had been carelessly tossed around by irresponsible participants. In this sense, and in this sense only, there was an army revolt, and it succeeded. To this extent Mackenzie King had not exaggerated the menace inherent in the situation on November 22, 1944.

While McNaughton had confided to another Minister on November 20 that he was sure that the voluntary system would produce the men and had told the Cabinet on November 21 that the system was by no means hopeless, he was no doubt nearer in his mind to its abandonment than he was willing to acknowledge. He had never said that he rejected conscription, indeed, he had said he might have to accept it, and his experience since assuming office had made this possibility appear more and more likely. He must therefore have received with mixed feelings the opportunity which was provided by the officers' memorandum to change his stand on the question. He had gone to the Department of Defence with little real appreciation of what lay ahead of him, and every day must have brought a new period of disillusionment. Not only was support from the army reluctantly forthcoming in many instances, but he was being abused and denounced by a substantial part of the press, and public opinion was giving his campaign little or no support. He had no knowledge of politics, no talent for political manoeuvring and compromise, and his experience in office, while short, had been both trying and discouraging. Enthusiasm and optimism, when not reinforced by such sterner qualities as a determination to fight back and a capacity to stand up in the general rough-and-tumble, could not carry him very far. The shabby parade of enlistment figures which appeared on his desk every morning would not be denied: where he had expected thousands from the N.R.M.A. ranks, he was receiving scanty hundreds. The McNaughton "crusade," in short, had up to this point not produced the overseas troops; and while a positive acknowledgment of that failure might still be postponed for a few weeks, awaiting a possible miracle in the British Columbia camps, there seemed little doubt but that that sorry admission would eventually have to be made.

It now appeared that the General was called upon not only to convert the recalcitrant men, but to work with high officers who to him at least were perverse, unco-operative, and disposed to throw in their resignations if they did not get their own way. How could he be expected to make the voluntary system work with such weak and tepid assistance? How could he face the Prime Minister, who had shown such confidence in him and had brought him into the Government to save the voluntary system, and admit, less than three weeks after he had taken office, that he could not produce the men?

How could he now meet the cold scepticism of some of his colleagues who had never believed in his ability to succeed where Ralston had failed? These and other similar considerations may well have led him to cast about, consciously, or not, for reasons which would make it easier to account for his inability to carry out his purpose, and, naturally enough, to exaggerate their potency. His disappointment and disillusionment, made more acute by his egocentricity and stimulated by a lambent imagination and a strong sense of theatre, thus encountered little difficulty in describing his troubles and his obstacles. The "blow in the stomach" dramatized both the unfairness of the attack and its calamitous effect on his position. Plottings, conspiracies, and revolts were, it seems, already present in his mind and they gained in stature and importance with each breach of discipline. The possible became the probable, and the danger of resignations and of the general disintegration of the service became magnified until it distorted his whole outlook for the future.

These may well have been the thoughts of the Minister on whom Mackenzie King largely depended for advice in military matters. King viewed the army from a remote eminence. He had little sympathy with it, virtually no direct contacts, and only a hazy understanding of its problems, and the failure of the Canadian headquarters in Europe to keep the Cabinet informed on reinforcements had placed it even lower in his esteem. He still had confidence in McNaughton; a belief which he must have found very difficult to retain, and one which was well nigh incredible except as a further example of King's tendency to idealize his appointments. In one way, however, this was a fortunate circumstance, for he was in no position after the Ralston dismissal to secure another adviser had he wished to do so. When McNaughton, the stalwart advocate of the voluntary system, advised its discontinuance, King was profoundly impressed and was at last prepared to accept the distasteful conclusion. Nor was he inclined to question the account McNaughton gave of the attitude of the army officers. His mind had been prepared for this kind of development by a number of McNaughton's earlier reports, and such public incidents as the press interviews in British Columbia and the resignation of the District Officer Commanding in Winnipeg formed part of a general pattern which was becoming increasingly distinct as the weeks elapsed.

It is probable that under different circumstances both King and McNaughton might have taken disciplinary measures to subdue this unrest in the army, even to the point of making the relations of the military to the civil power an election issue. But such action could not possibly be attempted at this time. Not only did the whole-hearted prosecution of the war have precedence over everything else, but virtually all of English-speaking Canada would have resented any such challenge to the army in wartime except as a last resort, and King would have been accused of arranging a political diversion to take the public attention off conscription. Any serious dispute with the army over its refusal to give warm support to what was the most controversial policy in the country would be most unwise; to risk it with a Cabinet torn by internal disagreement over the same policy would be utter folly. No Government could possibly have survived. King therefore accepted the lesser evil of conscription, which not only kept the army intact but also removed the danger of any conflict between the army and the Government.

But even when due allowance has been made for King's lack of confidence in the army and his dependence on McNaughton's advice in such matters, he was strangely willing to concur in his Minister's alarmist interpretation and he responded very quickly to the suggestion that the military machine would disintegrate unless drastic measures were adopted. It is quite possible that in view of the awkward situation which was developing from other quarters he was becoming increasingly uneasy as to his ability to defend his existing policy, an uneasiness made much more acute by the imminence of the parliamentary session. The trouble with the army not only furnished the final reason for his abandonment of the voluntary system, it also enabled him to justify to himself his change of front. He, like McNaughton, was witnessing the collapse of his cherished plans. He too was feeling both unhappy and frustrated, and he welcomed some extenuating circumstance which would lessen his discomfort and allow him to feel that no blame could be attached to himself. Where McNaughton was being forced to abandon a policy of three weeks' duration, King was deserting the convictions of a lifetime. For him to be the one to introduce conscription with its coercion of Quebec and its possible destruction of Canadian unity was almost unthinkable; he would thereby be forsaking a fundamental tenet of the Liberal party, violating the great tradition of Laurier, and turning away from a policy which he as leader had faithfully upheld and which had in no small measure been the secret of his political success. So complete a reversal could be satisfactorily explained and extenuated in his own mind only by magnifying the importance and impact of the circumstances which had brought it about. No mere rift in the Cabinet, no simple failure of voluntary enlistment, no trifling military lapses would suffice. The cause must be commensurate with the effect. Having dwelt so often on the emergency which alone would change his policy, it must be an emergency in the real sense of the word. "The soup he

took was Elephant soup, and the fish he took was Whale."
King's mind was instinctively searching for the catastrophic,
and it found a satisfactory answer in the threatened army
collapse, the possible conflict between the military power
and the Government, and the menace of civil war. Any
departure, no matter how unprecedented, could find its
justification in primary issues such as these, and he was
therefore disposed to exaggerate and not minimize them.
Unhappily at the time of the crisis he was forced by the
explosive nature of these circumstances to keep these
reasons almost entirely to himself, though in his own
thoughts he could still derive a profound consolation from
them. In later years when the need for reticence had disappeared, King did not hesitate to express his conviction
that these dangers had been very real indeed and that only
his prompt action had averted disaster.[33]

King's sudden decision on November 22, however, did not
rest alone on real or imaginary difficulties with the army. The
situation on the political front had been pushing him
reluctantly to the same conclusion. If he continued to support
the voluntary system the resignation of the conscriptionist
Ministers would be almost inevitable, and the ensuing crisis
would probably force him and the residue of the Cabinet
out of office. What then would follow might be uncertain
in detail, but he was bound to regard its general effect as
calamitous. A coalition of Liberal conscriptionists with one
or more of the Opposition parties would be formed; Quebec
would be isolated, and a national schism on racial lines,
already threatening, would be rapidly accelerated. The Liberal
party would again be torn apart. The effects of King's unremitting efforts of twenty-five years to rebuild and maintain
a united nation and a united party would be completely and
perhaps irrevocably destroyed.

If, on the other hand, the Government should accept conscription, the Prime Minister could count at the worst on the support of at least half of the Cabinet and he might do much better. There was a risk that all the Quebec Ministers might leave, but conceivably a number of them might be prepared to remain with the party which had always been sympathetic to the French Canadians. The chances of retaining the support of the Quebec members of Parliament was, however, not nearly so bright; for these members, whatever their own opinions might be, were deeply committed to their constituents on the vital issue. Few Quebec members would want to vote openly for conscription and they would be sure to find some allies from other provinces to swell their numbers in a division.

The long-range effects in the constituencies were also problematical. Conscription would undoubtedly be well received in most provinces, but Saskatchewan was considered doubtful and the Liberal losses in Quebec and other French districts might be heavy and irretrievable. Yet the severance of Quebec would be much less complete if the Liberals, rather than another party, took the responsibility for introducing conscription. Any Liberal gains (and these, by virtue of a late conversion, would be few) would be more than offset by losses in French-speaking areas where hitherto the party had been unusually strong. Its weakening hold on English Canada would be strengthened by conscription and would probably remain relatively unimpaired as a result of the change. Prophecy, however, was apt to be misleading. Public opinion was at the moment in such a state of flux that the eventual party alignment was hidden in uncertainties. The great consolation was that owing to the steady deterioration of the existing situation, a shift to conscription could do little harm and was likely to produce some general improvement.

These, however, were not the reasons which King publicly advanced to explain the Liberal support of conscription. He defended his action on the simple and obvious ground that conscription had become necessary because of the demonstrated inability of voluntary enlistment to produce the reinforcements. This failure, he argued, need not have occurred at all, but the demand for conscription had been so loud and persistent that it had in itself defeated the campaign for more recruits. The Government was faced with a shortage, and the only way now to fill the ranks was through conscription.[34] It was therefore prepared to pass the necessary Order-in-Council and compel the N.R.M.A. men to go overseas.

There is little reason to accept the above statement at its face value, for King was clearly trying to extricate himself from a situation which, while embarrassing, could not be fully explained. He obviously could not advertise the army's attitude or his misgivings in that direction, nor could he very well discuss the party's internal troubles and its outlook for the future. Had he been pressed to account more fully for his sudden switch, he would doubtless have added that the changes in the military and political situation during the preceding few weeks had made the adoption of conscription inevitable if a full war effort was to be maintained and the position of his Government secured.

The above account has given some indication of the complexity of the conscription issue and the number and variety of the pressures which entered into its solution. The growing certainty that the voluntary system was to prove inadequate within the time available; the insistence of a majority of Canadians that they would make no more concessions to the anti-conscriptionist minority; the weak co-operation and even hostility of the army; the threatened dissolution of the Cabinet and his own doubtful future as

Prime Minister; the threatened isolation of Quebec and its effect on national unity and the future of the Liberal party: these were all influential in helping King make up his mind. But above them all was his assured conviction that the national welfare in its widest sense depended on a united Canada, that the war effort must be considered as an indissoluble whole, and that even so vital a matter as the reinforcement of troops overseas could not be isolated entirely from the broader problem. In King's eyes this paramount national interest was completely identified with a united Liberal party, and hence the maintenance of that party in power under his own leadership was an essential condition precedent to effective action. With the sure intuitive judgment for which he was noted King responded to McNaughton's statement over the telephone; he realized instinctively that here he was being given a powerful argument which he could use to hold his Cabinet intact. His worries and uncertainties rolled away as the decision took shape in his mind. The interminable search for a solution was over. Confusion and uncertainty gave way to clarity; the endless balancing of argument and counter-argument became superfluous; the bewildering maze of alternatives which he had sought to penetrate for more than six weary weeks was replaced by a clear course which he saw stretching out straight before him.

THE *third* PHASE

The third and last phase of the conscription crisis centred about the events which followed the decision on the morning of November 22 and especially the manner in which King secured the adoption of his new policy of limited conscription. No time could be wasted, for Parliament was to meet that day and the Cabinet's policy had to be announced as soon as possible. King followed up the telephone conversation with McNaughton with a meeting with the General at Laurier House, but nothing occurred at that interview to alter King's decision. It was not possible, however, to submit the altered policy that afternoon to Parliament at its first sitting. The submission had to be made to Cabinet, caucus, and Parliament in that sequence; but unfortunately under arrangements which had already been made, the meetings were scheduled in exactly the reverse order to that named. The submission was therefore temporarily held in abeyance until it could be brought before each body at the appropriate time. The initial proceedings in Parliament and caucus were thereby rendered unreal and misleading. These bodies could not yet be told of what was impending, and no one but King and McNaughton was aware that the issue which was dominant in everybody's mind had, in effect, ceased to be an issue at all, at least in that particular context. Parliament on the afternoon of the 22nd did little more than receive the King–Ralston correspondence concerning the latter's resignation, although the Progressive-Conservatives tried to introduce a motion advocating conscription which was ruled out of order. A little later King spoke in the Liberal caucus on the reinforcement crisis, but he requested that any discussion on conscription should be postponed until the Cabinet had an opportunity to consider some fresh information which had just come to hand.

It was vital for King to obtain some assurance of Quebec support before he sprang his surprise on the Cabinet that evening. Accordingly as soon as he had left the caucus he sent for Mr. St. Laurent and told him of his interview with McNaughton and the decision he had made. St. Laurent was much perturbed at the picture King drew of a possible breakdown in the army and the risk of the country's being left without an effective staff or even without any staff at all, and the sincerity of King's apprehension is best gauged by the fact that he was apparently able to convince the level-headed Minister of Justice that the danger which he dreaded was a very real one. St. Laurent's natural inclination was to refuse to submit to anything which remotely resembled intimidation by the army, but he agreed with King that with a divided Cabinet they could not risk a major disagreement on this issue. As for conscription, while St. Laurent had hoped to finish the war without it, he was convinced that the maintenance of the infantry strength had become essential both because of its effect on morale and because of its supreme importance on the battlefield. If the voluntary system could not supply the men, he was willing to use compulsion. As he said a few days later: "I came here to do a war job, and because it was felt by the Prime Minister, rightly or wrongly, that I could be of some help, I feel I must still go on, whatever may be the increase in the difficulties of the task, so long as it is made apparent to me that these difficulties arise out of facts which have a bearing on the security of the men who are doing so much more for us than anything we can do for them."[1]

It will be remembered that Mr. St. Laurent had always endeavoured to keep an open mind on the conscription issue. Unlike every other French-Canadian Minister he had never at any time pledged himself as an anti-conscriptionist; indeed, he had said that compulsion might under some circumstances become unavoidable. In his talk with King, however, he took a very gloomy view of what the acceptance of conscription would mean in political terms. He considered that the Government would probably lose all the Quebec seats at the next election, and expected that he himself would be forced to retire from public life. He was nevertheless prepared to stand by the Prime Minister. His support at this moment was clearly of incalculable value to King as he prepared to face a troubled Cabinet, an unpredictable caucus, and later a wavering House. To the notable band of conscriptionists and the moderate group who would follow his leadership he could now add the one French-Canadian Minister who stood out far above his fellows. St. Laurent would not only bring his own prestige and ability to the new policy, his support would make precipitate action by the other Quebec Ministers most unlikely and his firmness might even be decisive in inducing them to stay with the Government.

While King was talking to St. Laurent a private meeting of conscriptionist Ministers was being held to discuss the course they should pursue in the immediate future. It was attended by Crerar, Ilsley, Macdonald, Howe, Gibson, and Mulock. The Cabinet, so far as these Ministers knew, would face Parliament the following day as the unregenerate supporters of the voluntary system, and none of this group of Ministers was willing to be placed in that position. After some discussion they agreed that they could no longer be responsible for the Government's policy and that each of them would therefore present his resignation to the Prime Minister forthwith. They broke up on that understanding. This meeting, incidentally, inspired one of the legends which grew up around the crisis. Mackenzie King, according to this story, had heard of the rebel gathering through an alleged spy system and as a result had switched to conscription between this meeting at five in the afternoon and the Cabinet meeting at eight that evening. The facts as narrated above show that the Prime Minister needed no such prolonged period in which to reverse his policy, and in fact had made the change as early as eleven o'clock that morning. But it is undeniable that he narrowly escaped having no Cabinet, or only a residue of a Cabinet, with which to face Parliament on the following day.

The "resignation meeting" of the Ministers is interesting not only because it indicates how high the feelings were running at this time but also because it shows how completely the dissenting Ministers had lost sight of the one vital issue to which they had hitherto given unquestioned priority, namely, the provision of essential reinforcements on time. They were convinced that conscription was the remedy and that King would not apply it, and thus, to maintain the narrow logic of their position, they must withdraw from the Cabinet. What would then ensue, they confessed they did not know. It could be argued that they were only trying to force the Prime Minister to act, to put a pistol to his head with no intention of pulling the trigger, but there is no evidence to bear out this supposition. If they did not expect Mackenzie King to capitulate before the threat of resignation, they were fully aware that the simultaneous withdrawal of six Ministers, including four of the first rank, would bring about an earthquake in the Cabinet. If the Cabinet survived, conscription would be postponed for some time. But if, as was more likely, the Cabinet fell, how much nearer would these Ministers be to the realization of their main purpose? Who would be Prime Minister? Where was the new Government to find its majority in the House? Would it immediately pass the necessary Order-in-Council? And if this new Government were formed, how could the debate in the House be conducted and a vote of confidence be obtained without a long delay? The Quebec members, at least, would never have suffered such changes passively and in silence. The people of that province would, as the facts later proved, take conscription with a fair grace from King's hand after their leaders in Parliament acquiesced, but there is no reason whatever to suppose that they would have done so if conscription had been imposed on them with the help of the rabid conscriptionist anti-Quebec faction which would have constituted an important part of any new conscriptionist Government. Moreover, by any fair estimate a majority in the House for such a Government was, at best, small: the opposition would be bitter and pugnacious, and a general election might well prove inescapable. It is difficult to see how all this could in any way promote the speedy dispatch of reinforcements; on the contrary, political uncertainties which were inherent in the situation would have compelled the postponement of any measures which could afford immediate relief. Even Ralston was constrained to acknowledge the reality of these political difficulties when confronted a few days later by the consequences which might follow a critical vote in the House. He said:

To vote for the amendment* is far more than registering [an] opinion. The amendment is, in fact, a motion of want of confidence because if it were carried, the Government's motion would be lost; and the Government, instead of driving ahead, . . . would cease to function, and the whole matter of dispatching these men, which I have so earnestly advocated, would be thrown into the realm of uncertainty and suspense. . . .

If the amendment were carried, I confess that I cannot, and I doubt if anyone can foresee clearly or with any reasonable certainty what would happen about the sending of these men. There would follow attempts to form a new Government, the probable necessity of any new Government having the assurance of the House, and the delays and uncertainties which are inevitable in a course of that kind. Or, instead of the formation of a new Government, there might be dissolution of the House and a general election. Either one of these alternatives, while some people might regard them as preferable to the present situation, would constitute in my judgment a definite deterrent to the quick dispatch of these reinforcements. That action . . . is at the moment the supreme consideration.[2]

Mackenzie King had been on solid ground when in October he had repeatedly asked the dissatisfied Ministers how another Government could overcome the problem of urgency which would be rendered more intractable by the political difficulties that would be called into being by the creation of the new Government itself. The only person who could apply conscription without involving endless delays

*[The amendment referred to was moved on November 27 by the Progressive-Conservatives (Graydon moving, Diefenbaker the seconder); its purpose was to insert into King's motion (see *supra*, p. 116) after "That" the words: "this House is of the opinion that the government has not made certain of adequate and continuous trained reinforcements by requiring all N.R.M.A. personnel whether now or hereafter enrolled to serve in any theatre of war and has failed to assure equality of service and sacrifice."—EDITORIAL NOTE.]

and obstacles was King, and while the dissenting Ministers might dislike him and suspect his methods, that hostility in no way destroyed the essential fact that without his co-operation and support the desired results could not be secured. Well might King at this time have repeated Chatham's arrogant statement: "I know that I can save this nation and that no one else can."

Before meeting the Cabinet that evening King had a talk with another Quebec Minister, C. G. Power. This was not as successful as that with St. Laurent. He told Power that the lack of volunteers made it imperative to pass an Order-in-Council immediately to send 16,000 N.R.M.A. men overseas. He appealed to Power to stay with the Government and laid special stress on the close friendship which had always existed between them. He also emphasized the necessity for maintaining a Government in Canada and the difficulty or even impossibility of keeping anything but a Liberal administration in office at this time. Power was far from convinced that the gravity of the crisis justified so drastic a remedy, and he thought that the public had become emotionally overwrought in its attitude to the existing situation. He was particularly concerned with the damage which compulsion would inflict on national unity. Admittedly King's proposal might be successful in holding the Government together, but his own attitude had been so definite that he felt he had no choice but to leave the Cabinet if it decided to take the final step.

A few minutes after this interview King made his announcement to a full Cabinet. General McNaughton, he said, had reported that morning that "the voluntary system of recruiting through Army channels cannot meet the immediate problem," and he therefore proposed that a limited number of N.R.M.A. troops should be taken to fill up the reinforcement pool. King said that he reluctantly supported the General's

recommendation, and asked for its most careful consideration. The response by the Cabinet was, in view of past disagreements, surprisingly favourable. Some attention was once
again given to other alternatives, notably to an ingenious but
complicated draft scheme of Claxton's, based on enlistment
quotas, which had been discussed at the last meeting.
It was quickly apparent, however, that conscription would
be accepted by most of the Ministers without serious protest,
either from conviction, or as a way out of a situation which
was rapidly becoming intolerable, or as the only solution
which would be able to hold the Cabinet together. King
made no mention whatever of the anticipated trouble with
the army if the existing system were retained. Leaks in Cabinet proceedings had been all too frequent, and he naturally
feared the consequences if the rumour became current that
the Government had little confidence in the army's relia-
bility or that many officers in the army would not continue
to give their support to Government policies.

The general acquiescence of the Cabinet having been
established, King proposed that the caucus should not meet
until after McNaughton had made his statement to the
House. This brought a passionate protest from St. Laurent
who pointed out that the Quebec Ministers would need all
the support they could muster, and to push the caucus to one
side in this fashion would be utter folly. Although King's
proposal had been in accord with the usual procedure, he
at once concurred in St. Laurent's suggestion, and he agreed
to address the caucus the next day.

During these proceedings the Quebec Ministers said
little. They were acutely unhappy at the turn of events
and most of them were undecided on their future course.
King's great effort at this time, as on many other occasions,
was to prevent any Minister from taking a sudden step
which after greater deliberation he might regret, and he

made a fervent appeal for moderation and Cabinet unity. Power, however, announced that he would have to resign, and Gardiner said that in that event he would go as well. King spoke again and said that if Ministers began to drop out, he himself would have to leave, that he could not fight enemies in his own household. A collapse of the Government during the war would inflict tremendous damage on the country and the war effort. He begged Power and Gardiner to remain at their posts at least until the next day. He then quickly closed the meeting.

Following the Cabinet discussion, King sent for St. Laurent and two other Quebec Ministers, Bertrand and Fournier. He thanked them for staying with him and begged them to remain united with the rest of the Cabinet. He then talked with McNaughton about the General's address for the following day. McNaughton had, of course, no seat in Parliament, but the House had decided to allow him to appear on the floor, give his address, and reply to questions. The circumstances surrounding the *début* of this inexperienced parliamentarian were not the most favourable, for the unfortunate General was compelled to transform a maiden speech which had just been written to support the voluntary system into a defence of limited conscription. The task began at midnight under the General's direction, and King's secretarial staff toiled diligently until five o'clock in the morning, rewriting and adapting the speech so that a reasoned defence of voluntary enlistment was transformed under their hands into a convincing argument for conscription.

King retired shortly after midnight. It had been a full day. The disturbing telephone conversation with General McNaughton, the critical decision to accept conscription at once, the further discussion with McNaughton, King's attendance at and active participation in Parliament and the caucus, the crucial interview with St. Laurent and the later one with Power, the supremely important Cabinet meeting, followed by other interviews—these were far from being matters of routine. They were of the utmost consequence to the country's future and to King personally; they all made extraordinary demands on his power of persuasion, his gifts of leadership, his nervous energy, and his vitality. The same day's schedule had also allowed him to do his usual devotional reading, to write a letter, to hold a number of minor conferences, and to make preparations for his parliamentary duties. Mackenzie King was now less than a month away from his seventieth birthday. He had been in office continuously since 1935; he had been Prime Minister for more than five years of war; he had just come through a terrific five weeks and was in the midst of his second crisis in that period. The Cabinet had been divided and was still uncertain, many of his most cherished policies were being shelved, and the outlook was clouded with doubt. Yet except for a nosebleed when he got home that night he was unruffled and was conscious of little fatigue. Somehow during that eventful day he had also contrived to secure two rest periods of twenty minutes each, and to dictate on two separate occasions a number of pages in his diary. "To-day has gone well," he wrote serenely. "Tomorrow will be very difficult and the following day possibly most difficult of all. But I believe the right decision has been reached."[8] To this must be added the opening sentence of the diary for the next day: "On the whole, I slept very well last night."

The following morning King arose refreshed to face the great ordeal. At this time he had a special reason to follow his customary practice of preparing for the day's work through a period of religious devotion. It was typical that in this supreme crisis of his life he should turn to Christian sources of inspiration and comfort. He did so, not only as a Christian, but also as a profoundly lonely man in dire straits. The basic loneliness which flowed from the absence of a family and intimate friends was deepened by the self-imposed isolation which must be the fate of all prime ministers. He felt a desperate need for divine support, and was eager to discover direct evidence of it. Even a sceptic cannot fail to be struck by the manner in which the evidence frequently responded to his need. On this occasion it did not fail him. Opening first his favourite religious anthology, *Daily Strength for Daily Needs*, at the page for November 23, he found there:

"We have very little command over the circumstances in which we may be called by God to bear our part—unlimited command over the temper of our souls, but next to no command over the outward forms of trial. The most energetic will cannot order the events by which our spirits are to be perilled and tested. Powers quite beyond our reach—death, accident, fortune, another's sin—may change in a moment all the conditions of our life. With to-morrow's sun existence may have new and awful aspects for any of us."—J. H. THOM

"Oh, my friend, look not *out* at what stands in the way; what if it look dreadfully as a lion, is not the Lord stronger than the mountains of prey? but look *in*, where the law of life is written, and the will of the Lord revealed, that thou mayest know what is the Lord's will concerning thee."—I. PENINGTON

He next turned to his *Devotional Diary* of scriptural quotations for the same date, which he described in his own diary later in the day as follows:

The first line [of the *Devotional Diary*] was "they crucified Him." All week I have been looking forward to today being one of the most difficult days in my life and one which would mean that I would be between bitter opposing forces. I confess I derived some comfort from the thought that one was truly following the example of Christ in facing the situation without fear and with some vision of what lies beyond an experience of the kind. The fuller life which comes in time when principle has been held to the extremity of endurance.

In reading the 14th chapter of Zechariah, I also found something most needed for to-day in the conclusion of the chapter: "And I will bring the third part through the fire, and I will refine them as silver is refined, and will try them as gold is tried; they shall call on my name, and I will hear them: I will say, It is my people: And they shall say, The Lord is My God." All through there has been the conviction that this experience is part of the refining process.* It was that test that has stood out at the beginning. It is remarkable that it should appear in the reading today.

I prayed very earnestly for strength guidance and courage today.[4]

The reference to the Crucifixion can be appreciated only by realizing that for weeks past he had been seeking reassurance from the story of Christ's life and had found comfort in drawing a parallel between Christ's suffering and endurance and his own immediate extremity.† This identification of experiences satisfied his need: it confirmed his certainty of virtue and high purpose; and he derived great comfort from dwelling on the misunderstanding and misrepresentation which underlay the activities of his enemies. He felt blameless and misjudged, a sacrifice in the cause of righteousness, one who was called upon to undergo the supreme ordeal while sustained by the certain hope of the resurrection to come.

Thus fortified, King plunged into the business of the day. The draft Order-in-Council was read and altered, and

---

*This reference had already appeared in the diary on October 29 and November 14, and it reappeared on November 24.

†There are no less than twelve references to his experience and some phase of Christ's Passion in his diary between October 29 and November 25. Six of these occur in the days November 23–5.

General McNaughton's speech, diligently beaten out during the night, was carefully scrutinized and some revisions made after a telephone conversation with the Minister.

King then looked to his newspaper defences. He called up McConnell of the Montreal *Star*, Atkinson of the Toronto *Star*, and Grant Dexter of the Winnipeg *Free Press*, all of whom had long been his staunch supporters but had unmistakably wavered during the past few weeks. Without giving them any definite information, he assured them that they would be satisfied with the Government's decision on reinforcements, and suggested that they should withhold further criticism until they had heard what the Government proposed.

He next turned his attention to Quebec. He telephoned Cardinal Villeneuve and told him that a limited measure of conscription was inevitable. The Cardinal said that while he had hoped to avoid conscription he could appreciate the political difficulties, and he indicated that he would see what he could do to be helpful. King also called Adelard Godbout, ex-Premier of Quebec, and informed him of the Government's intentions, but he received only a non-committal response.

Before King left for the caucus meeting he was informed that letters from two Ministers, Power and Gardiner, were at his office. He suspected that they might contain resignations, and he decided to ignore them for the time. He would doubtless hear about them soon enough.

When the Prime Minister entered the caucus he was given a tremendous ovation by the members and senators who filled the room to the doors. He lost no time in beginning his story. It took over an hour. He outlined the history of the conscription issue and the events leading up to the decision of the previous evening, omitting, however, any reference to anticipated trouble in the army. The public campaign for men had apparently failed, and time was running out. The solution proposed was a compromise: the conscription of a limited number of N.R.M.A. men. The party was now united. Let it not break up at this late date, but let each be prepared to surrender some ground and avoid resignations and adverse votes which might defeat the Government. Power then interjected that he was not in agreement with the Cabinet on this new departure and he had written King and told him that he could accept no responsibility for it. Gardiner also added a protest and stated that he too had sent a letter to the Prime Minister. King said that he had not received their letters, and turned the interruptions to advantage by citing them as illustrations of the danger he had just mentioned. If he were confronted with any substantial number of desertions, he would have no choice but to relinquish the prime ministership. The lot of the anti-conscriptionists would then become hopeless, for a new Government would almost certainly demand complete conscription and apply it not to the European theatre alone, but possibly to the Far East as well. Each member, however, must make his decision on his own responsibility.

When King had concluded his speech, Gardiner elaborated his position and made it clear that he had not resigned but was simply dissatisfied with some of the steps which were being taken. Ralston, whose withdrawal from the Cabinet had of course not affected his membership in the House or the caucus, followed with a fairly long speech. He drew especial attention to his advocacy of compulsion a few weeks before and reaffirmed his own Liberal tradition and his continuing belief in Liberalism. Both Gardiner's and Ralston's speeches, King considered, were helpful rather than antagonistic. If he had ever entertained any doubts about Ralston's willingness to support the Government's conscription proposals, they must have been set at rest by this display of magnanimity and moderation. Throughout the proceedings the Quebec members, who were naturally the hardest hit, appeared distressed and anxious—some looked grim and determined—but they stood silent. The blow had at last fallen. If they protested and threatened, they cut themselves off from the Government, their only sure defender, and might be compelled to accept a much more unsympathetic successor; if they acquiesced, they faced almost certain vengeance at the hands of their constituents, whom they had assured, time without number, that they would never be a party to the imposition of conscription. Silence, for the moment at least, committed them to nothing. The Prime Minister, for his part, was only too anxious to give them ample time for reflection and discussion among themselves before they made up their minds and took a definitive stand in the presence of their colleagues. He therefore had the caucus adjourn immediately after Ralston's speech.

A short Cabinet meeting followed. King was dreading another debate on the terms of the proposed Order-in-Council now that it had taken tangible form, but the discussion proved to be brief and was confined to details. The Order departed from the Government's earlier promise that if conscription was adopted it would be applied to all eligibles, but the Cabinet agreed that it was wiser to limit the first draft to 16,000 men, although it should be made quite clear that the Government was prepared to apply further Orders-in-Council to conscript more men for overseas service if conditions should so require. In the middle of the discussion Power left the meeting. He handed his written resignation to the Prime Minister, shook hands with him and wished him luck, and said a general good-bye to his colleagues. A few minutes later, King signed the Order-in-Council.[5] He was relieved to find that no one tried to follow Power, and he once more gained a reprieve for himself and a period of reflection for any dissatisfied Ministers by speedily breaking up the Cabinet meeting.

It lacked but fifteen minutes to the meeting of Parliament. King had a chicken sandwich and a cup of tea, and took his place in the House for his third major engagement of the day.

King's part in this day's sitting, however, was relatively small, for even with his skilful use of time he had been unable to find an opportunity to prepare his speech for Parliament. He therefore said little. He read the Order-in-Council, and observed with satisfaction the discomfiture of the Opposition, who saw the whole power of their attack vanish in the course of a few minutes. The quarry which they thought had at last been run to earth was off again in a clear field, and all they could do was to resume the chase and see the gap between pursuer and pursued widen once more. General McNaughton, appearing on the sufferance of the House, was allowed to speak and answer questions, and he therefore bore the major load at this time. In view of his complete lack of parliamentary experience he did fairly well, and the Prime Minister was there to come to his rescue when matters threatened to get out of control.

The motion of confidence in the Government was moved by Mackenzie King on November 27.* It was a surprisingly good effort.⁶ He had had inadequate time for preparation, and even his powers of endurance were beginning to flag, but he was fighting for his political life and once more he showed his ability to draw on his reserves to meet an emergency. He began by reviewing in detail the Government's

*[The motion read: "That this House will aid the government in its policy of maintaining a vigorous war effort." See *supra*, p. 83.— EDITORIAL NOTE.]

policy on the raising of troops since the outbreak of war. The voluntary system, he said, had been pushed as far as it could go, it had failed to produce the men, and limited conscription would therefore be necessary to raise the reinforcements.[7] He was struck by the parallel between the existing situation and that in the province of Canada before Confederation when Sir John Macdonald feared "impending anarchy" as a result of an excessive particularism and a refusal to compromise. The sharp and apparently irreconcilable opinions today also threatened to destroy any Government which might be formed, and the consequences might be far more disastrous than many realized.

[The major issue at the moment] is not the question of conscription; it is the question of whether the present Government should continue to conduct Canada's war effort, or whether the direction of that effort should be handed over at this stage of the war to another administration. In destroying the present Government no one can tell who will compose an alternative Government. . . . A considerable number of the Ministers in such a Government would inevitably be new men without experience of our war-time administration. . . . Dislocations and delays in every aspect of our war administration would be bound to be serious at this critical stage of the war. But it would be even more serious if it were found, after the present Government had been defeated, that the various elements which had combined to destroy it were incapable of agreeing upon an effective Government to replace it. . . . An election would be inevitable, and what would happen to Canada's magnificent war effort while an election of probably unparalleled bitterness was being fought?[8]

The resignation of his Government would naturally follow the defeat of the motion of confidence. Realizing the uncertainties in the minds of many of his own followers, he made a passionate appeal for their votes. Turning his back on the Speaker and the Opposition and facing the Liberal rank and file he reminded Quebec how he had sought to have the rest of Canada understand its special needs and how he had always tried to protect their rights against any unreasonable demands by the majority. He would not, he said, be prepared to carry on as Prime Minister unless he could obtain "enough support out of my own party to feel sure that the men of my own party are behind me without depending on those who are politically opposed." At the opening of his speech he had avowed that the maintenance of national unity had been "above all else, the purpose of my work in Public life," and he ended on the same note by quoting the words of Sir Wilfrid Laurier and applying them to his record and to himself:

If there is anything to which I have devoted my political life, it is to try to promote unity, harmony and amity between the diverse elements of this country. My friends can desert me, they can remove their confidence from me, they can withdraw the trust they have placed in my hands, but never shall I deviate from that line of policy. Whatever may be the consequences, whether loss of prestige, loss of popularity, or loss of power, I feel that I am in the right, and I know that a time will come when every man will render me full justice on that score.[9]

The unknown factor in the early stages of the debate was the attitude of the French Canadians. It was soon evident that this vote would split, though emotions and loyalties were so mixed that little could be forecast with certainty. Some speakers, especially those who were determined to go down fighting under the now tattered banner of anti-conscription, were anxious to bring this to their constituents' attention, while others clearly preferred to acquiesce silently in the inevitable. King worked diligently behind the scenes, first, to hold his Cabinet intact, and second, to prevent the French-Canadian members from voting with his opponents. Once Power had resigned, the only doubtful Ministers were the French Canadians, and on the whole they gave King little cause for uneasiness. One of the least of them, however, remained irresolute for days; but after a sojourn in bed and a period of lurking behind the curtains of the House he resumed his seat and was ironically welcomed back by the Opposition. With this momentary lapse the Cabinet held firm.

King's approach to Ministers and members alike was to beseech them to take their time and reflect on the alternatives before them, especially the consequences which might follow a defeat of the Government. He displayed great patience at all times, and showed more sympathy than annoyance when a member felt compelled to come to an adverse decision. Three Quebec Liberals crossed the floor of the House during the debate, but the remainder, whatever their vote on the crucial question was to be, took no overt step to sever their party relations.

The diversity of views among the French Canadians may be illustrated by a brief reference to the speeches of three of the most prominent. P. J. A. Cardin saw in the Order-in-Council a confirmation of the fears which he had expressed when he left the Cabinet over the terms of Bill 80, and he ascribed the existing difficulties to inefficient planning and the over-expansion of the Canadian forces. He announced his intention of voting against the motion.

Mr. Hugues Lapointe, recently returned from active service, stated that he also would vote against the Government, and the reasons he gave for so doing were shared by a large number of his compatriots. "I believe," he said, "I truly express the sentiments of the people whom I have the honour to represent here when I tell the Prime Minister that there is no one else whom they want to see as the head of the Government of Canada, but on the other hand they cannot forget the breaking of a pledge which to them was sacred. I hope, Mr. Speaker, that the task to which the Prime Minister has devoted his whole life, and the national unity which he succeeded in realizing in Canada, will not come to an end because of the present issue."[10] This was by far the most effective speech made against the motion. It was a fine effort in itself, and as it was made by a soldier and the son of Ernest Lapointe it carried great additional weight. King referred in his diary to this as "an entirely sincere speech and a very brave and courageous one" although he acknowledged that it had hurt him more than anything else in the debate. "I know what a searching of soul his speech had cost him," he added. "I can understand his position and I would be the last not to make every allowance for it."[11]

The general policy of the Government had been to keep the Ministers out of the debate, but Lapointe's speech threatened to unsettle the Quebec members and made some answer on behalf of the Government inescapable. Mr. St. Laurent was selected for this purpose. "We could not afford," the Prime Minister told the Cabinet, "to allow the French members who are wishing to support the Government not to have before them the ground stated by one of their own Ministers on which it should be supported. Otherwise we were letting Lapointe become the voice of Quebec in voting against the administration. . . . Both for the present and the future of Quebec it was imperative that the senior member of the province should speak and give the grounds on which the Government's war policy should be supported."[12] Mr. St. Laurent defended the Government's policy on the existing need for reinforcements, and he pleaded for the acquiescence of the minority in the decision submitted by the Cabinet. He pointed out that democratic government in Canada, more than in most countries, would be successful only by recog-

nizing certain conventional restraints in the troubled area
of minority and majority rights. He said:

The will of the majority must be respected and it must prevail.
But I trust that, here in Canada, the majority will always, as it
is doing in this case, assert that will only after giving due consideration to the feelings and views of the minority and to the
reasons for such feelings and views, and then only to the extent
to which the majority is sincerely convinced that the general
interests of the whole body politic require that it be thus
asserted.[14]

The general level of debate among the Opposition members
was not high. The Progressive-Conservatives, having been deprived of their heaviest weapon by the Order-in-Council,
were inclined to fall back on captious criticism of details
and on the general complaint that partial conscription was
neither fair nor efficient. The C.C.F. again advanced their
demands for the compulsory mobilization of all resources,
material as well as human, and the Social Credit party displayed its peculiar genius by utilizing this opportunity, like
all others, to give obscure expression to their monetary ideas.

Unusual attention was given to Ralston's speech. The
prominent part he had played in the crisis had added to his
already impressive stature in the House and it was not
impossible that his attitude on the motion might affect the
final result. He spoke with his usual sincerity and forceful-
ness.[15] For the first time he gave the House his version of
the manpower crisis, and he discussed in detail the disagreement which had led to his withdrawal from the Cabinet. He
disapproved of the "half-hearted piecemeal method" now
proposed, but he had no qualms in voting to sustain the
Government. "Action," he said, "is more important than
method," and the men would get overseas more quickly
and more certainly if the House would give an affirmative

verdict. Ralston was not seeking any petty revenge on the Prime Minister: his overwhelming concern was still to reinforce the army overseas. Such a pronouncement from this source virtually ensured that all English-speaking Liberals would support King's motion. Ralston's attitude, after his stand at the Liberal caucus, was no surprise to his own party; but the disappointed expression on many faces in the Opposition showed that they had misjudged Ralston's character and exaggerated the gap which now existed between his position and that of the Government.

As the debate went into its second week it was obvious that the Government could count on obtaining a substantial majority. King had received early promises from the Social Credit party that its members would vote for his motion, and on December 7 he secured also the support of the C.C.F. by accepting their amendment to drop the words "its policy of" from the resolution "That this House will aid the Government in its policy of maintaining a vigorous war effort." The amended motion was carried on December 7 by a vote of 143 to 70,[16] the minority being an incongruous combination of Progressive-Conservatives, a few die-hard isolationists from Quebec, and a number of Quebec representatives who were not prepared to support the motion. A breakdown of the French-Canadian vote shows that 23 voted for King's motion (13 from Quebec, 10 from other provinces) and 34 voted against it, all but one of whom came from Quebec. Nine French Canadian constituencies, eight of which were in Quebec, either were vacant or their members did not vote. Mackenzie King might well be content with the result:

If ever a Government had to steer a course between Charybdis and Scylla, it was the present Administration during the months of October and November. I shall never be able to say how grateful I was and ever will be to my colleagues of French origin who kept so close to my side as we ran into and safely beyond the cataract which threatened to engulf us all. I believe history will affirm that no stronger bond of national unity betwen the French and English provinces of Canada has ever been forged. It may take a little time for the people to realize this, but I am quite sure that posterity will.[17]

The defection of the thirty-four French Canadian Liberals, however, did not mean any permanent weakening of the party's strength in Parliament. Even before the vote was taken King had expressions of goodwill and continuing cooperation on all other matters from many members of this group. They had given such explicit pledges against conscription to their constituents that no matter how desirous they might have been to support King on the vote of confidence they could not do so. They realized, however, that if conscription had to come, its administration under Liberal auspices would be conducted with sympathy and understanding. King embodied this Liberal tradition to a unique degree and they therefore trusted him as they trusted no other English-speaking leader to defend the identity of their culture and its position in Canadian life.

Moreover, King's conduct of affairs in recent weeks had strongly reinforced his position in French Canada. He had dismissed Ralston to avoid the disintegration of his Cabinet and to postpone a final judgment on the adequacy of the voluntary system. The effects of this action, however, extended far beyond the achievement of these relatively narrow purposes and they were to a large degree unexpected. Ralston appeared inevitably in French-Canadian eyes as the one man in the Cabinet who was responsible for the army and who was likely to try to force them overseas. Conscription had always meant to them the domination of the Anglo-Saxon. Ralston was the leader of the conscriptionist wing of the Cabinet, and Ralston, therefore, had become the unwitting symbol for the oppressor of the minority. The shattering of this symbol satisfied the deep unvoiced demands of French Canada for a sacrifice, and much of the extreme bitterness which had surrounded the question disappeared. On more rational grounds, the dismissal was a very practical demonstration of how far King was willing to go to meet anti-conscriptionist feeling, and when, under the new Minister, the necessary reinforcements were still not forthcoming, the way was open for the adoption of compulsion as the only practicable alternative.

Thus when the House adjourned on December 7, 1944, there were few members who did not look back on the last days of the session with some feeling of satisfaction, and even the French Canadians experienced on the whole profound relief. Conscription had not only been adopted as a remedy for an exigent situation, it had been put forward by the majority in such a fashion and under such circumstances that the minority could accept it, if not with enthusiasm, at least with a substantial degree of goodwill. The contrast with 1917 was inescapable. The horrible vision had been confronted and its evil visage was recognized as being in large part the product of an unreasoning fear. The ghost of conscription was again laid, this time perhaps for ever, and the chief exorcist was Mackenzie King.

There are many Canadians who believe that in the King–Ralston struggle, Ralston emerged as the final victor, inasmuch as the conscription policy which he advocated was accepted within a few weeks of his dismissal. Such an interpretation is superficial, for it ignores the vital importance of timing. What could be done successfully on November 22 would have been disastrous if attempted three weeks earlier. For it was in that interval that the French-speaking minority was presented with a compelling demonstration that the majority, under the leadership of Mackenzie King, was not bent on making conscription an issue of naked power. The French minority responded to this restraint by waiving their former reluctance to allow the majority will to prevail, and by that acquiescence removed the one great barrier to conscription. Political decisions in a democracy can never be dissociated from popular consent. It is not enough for the wisest Government to decide on a course of action unless it can rely on the effective co-operation of its people; and the more vital and controversial the issue, the more essential is it that this co-operation be whole-hearted and extend beyond the mere limits of majority rule.

notes

THE *first* PHASE

1. J. L. Ralston, *Can. H. of C. Debates*, Nov. 29, 1944, p. 6663.
2. C. P. Stacey, *The Canadian Army, 1939–1945* (Ottawa: Queen's Printer, 1948), p. 233.
3. *Can. H. of C. Debates*, Nov. 23, 1944, pp. 6539, 6545.
4. *Ibid.*, Nov. 27, 1944, p. 6600.
5. *Ibid.*, Nov. 29, 1944, p. 6660.
6. *Ibid.*, July 10, 1944, p. 4657.
7. *Ibid.*, Nov. 27, 29, 1944, pp. 6598, 6660.
8. Stacey, *The Canadian Army, 1939–1945*, p. 234.
9. *Can. H. of C. Debates*, Nov. 29, 1944, p. 6662.
10. *Ibid.*, Nov. 27, 1944, p. 6598.
11. R. S. Malone, *Missing from the Record* (Toronto, 1946), p. 161.
12. Stacey, *The Canadian Army, 1939–1945*, pp. 233–4. *Can. H. of C. Debates*, Nov. 29, 1944, pp. 6667–72.
13. Diary, Oct. 18, 1944.
14. *Can. H. of C. Debates*, June 10, 1942, p. 3234.
15. *Ibid.*, Nov. 27, 1944, p. 6601.
16. *Ibid.*, June 10, 1942, p. 3239.
17. *Ibid.*, p. 3240.
18. Diary, Dec. 11, 1941.
19. *Can. H. of C. Debates*, July 10, 1944, p. 4659; Diary, Oct. 18, 1944.

20. Diary, Oct. 22, 1944.
21. *Ibid.*, Oct. 21, 1944.
22. *Ibid.*, Oct. 20, 25, 26, 27, 28, 30, Nov. 1, 1944.
23. *Ibid.*, Oct. 25, 26, 30, 31, 1944.
24. Montreal *Gazette*, Oct. 23, 1944.
25. Diary, Oct. 24, 1944.
26. *Can. H. of C. Debates*, Nov. 27, 29, 1944, pp. 6603, 6663–4.
27. Diary, Nov. 1, 1944.
28. *Ibid.*
29. *Ibid.* See also *Can. H. of C. Debates*, Nov. 27, 1944, pp. 6602–3.
30. Diary, Nov. 1, 1944.
31. *Can. H. of C. Debates*, Nov. 27, 1944, p. 6602.
32. *Ibid.*
33. *Ibid.*, Nov. 22, 1944, p. 6506.
34. *Ibid.*, Nov. 29, 1944, p. 6664.
35. Diary, Nov. 2, 1944.

THE *second* PHASE

1. Toronto *Globe and Mail*, Nov. 3, 1944 (edit.).
2. E.g., Winnipeg *Free Press*, Nov. 2, 3, 1944 (edit.).
3. *Le Soleil*, Oct. 30, 1944, reprinted in Toronto *Globe and Mail*, Nov. 1, 1944.
4. Diary, Oct. 31, Nov. 1, 1944.
5. *Can. H. of C. Debates*, Nov. 23, 1944, p. 6543.
6. Montreal *Gazette*, Nov. 13, 1944.
7. Diary, Nov. 13, 1944.
8. *Le Devoir*, Nov. 6, 1944 (trans.).
9. Toronto *Globe and Mail*, Nov. 16, 1944.
10. Montreal *Gazette*, Nov. 22, 1944.
11. *Ibid.*, Nov. 22, 1944.
12. *Can. H. of C. Debates*, Nov. 23, 1944, p. 6519.
13. *Ibid.*, Nov. 29, 1944, p. 6675.
14. *Ibid.*, p. 6674.
15. *Ottawa Journal*, Nov. 16, 1944.
16. Diary, Nov. 19, 1944.
17. Toronto *Globe and Mail*, Nov. 21, 1944.
18. Minute of Morning Army Conference, Nov. 19, 1944 (McNaughton Papers).
19. Toronto *Globe and Mail*, Nov. 21, 1944.

20. Montreal *Gazette*, Dec. 14, 1944.
21. Wartime Information Board, *Survey*, Nov. 18, 1944.
22. Toronto *Globe and Mail*, Nov. 7, 1944.
23. *Ibid.*, Nov. 7, 1944.
24. Diary, Nov. 9, 1944.
25. *Can. H. of C. Debates*, Nov. 23, 1944, pp. 6519, 6542–3.
26. Diary, Nov. 21, 1944.
27. *Ibid.*, Nov. 21, 1944.
28. *Ibid.*, Nov. 22, 1944.
29. *Ibid.*, Nov. 13, 19, 20, 1944.
30. Vancouver *Province*, Nov. 20, 1944.
31. *Ibid.*, Nov. 24, 1944.
32. Bruce Hutchison, *The Incredible Canadian* (Toronto, 1952), pp. 374–5, 380–3.
33. M. Freedman, "Mr. Mackenzie King," Winnipeg *Free Press*, Dec. 20, 1952.
34. *Can. H. of C. Debates*, Nov. 27, 1944, pp. 6594–610.

THE *third* PHASE

1. *Can. H. of C. Debates*, Dec. 6, 1944, pp. 6859–60.
2. *Ibid.*, Nov. 29, 1944, pp. 6676–7.
3. Diary, Nov. 22, 1944.
4. *Ibid.*, Nov. 23, 1944.
5. The text is found in *Can. H. of C. Debates*, Nov. 23, 1944, p. 6516.
6. *Ibid.*, Nov. 27, 1944, pp. 6594–618.
7. *Supra*, p. 115.
8. *Can. H. of C. Debates*, Nov. 27, 1944, p. 6611.
9. *Ibid.*, pp. 6617–18.
10. *Ibid.*, Dec. 5, 1944, p. 6831.
11. Diary, Dec. 5, 1944.
12. *Ibid.*, Dec. 6, 1944.
13. *Can. H. of C. Debates*, Dec. 6, 1944, p. 6860.
14. *Ibid.*, Nov. 29, 1944, pp. 6657–79.
15. *Ibid.*, Dec. 7, 1944, pp. 6952–3.
16. W.L.M.K. to Thomas Vien, Dec. 28, 1944.

appendix

THE MACKENZIE KING MINISTRY
SEPTEMBER 1, 1944–DECEMBER 7, 1944

SEPTEMBER 1, 1944

Prime Minister, President of the Privy Council, and Secretary of State for External Affairs	W. L. Mackenzie King
Leader of the Government in the Senate	J. H. King
Minister of Mines and Resources	T. A. Crerar
Minister of Justice	Louis S. St. Laurent
Minister of Public Works	Alphonse Fournier
Minister of Finance	J. L. Ilsley
Postmaster General	W. P. Mulock
Minister of Trade and Commerce	James A. MacKinnon
Secretary of State of Canada	Norman A. McLarty
Minister of National Defence	J. L. Ralston
Associate Minister of National Defence	Charles G. Power
Minister of National Defence for Air	Charles G. Power
Minister of National Defence for Naval Services	Angus L. Macdonald
Minister of Pensions and National Health	Ian A. Mackenzie
Minister of National Revenue	Colin Gibson
Minister of Fisheries	Ernest Bertrand
Minister of Labour	Humphrey Mitchell
Minister of Transport	J. E. Michaud
Minister of Munitions and Supply	C. D. Howe
Minister of Agriculture	James G. Gardiner
Minister of National War Services	L. R. LaFlèche

CHANGES

OCTOBER 13, 1944

IAN A. MACKENZIE became Minister of *Veterans Affairs*, the office of Minister of Pensions and National Health having been abolished

BROOKE CLAXTON became Minister of *National Health and Welfare*

C. D. HOWE became Minister of *Reconstruction* as well as of Munitions and Supply

NOVEMBER 2, 1944

A. G. L. McNAUGHTON became Minister of *National Defence*, succeeding J. L. Ralston

NOVEMBER 26, 1944

CHARLES G. POWER resigned as Associate Minister of National Defence and Minister of National Defence for Air

NOVEMBER 30, 1944

ANGUS L. MACDONALD became *Acting Minister of National Defence for Air*, following the resignation of Charles G. Power

index

Lightning Source UK Ltd.
Milton Keynes UK
UKHW012359200722
406167UK00001B/287